MW01273842

"May **True Healing** be a blessing to all who read it for healing the wound of the heart".

—**Bob Stahl**, co-author of *A Mindfulness-Based Stress Reduction Workbook,* and senior teacher for the Oasis Institute for Mindfulness-Based Professional Education

"**True Healing** is a brilliant and beautifully written exploration of sickness as a sacred passage. Drawing on her own descent into the depths of a seemingly incurable condition, Alison shares her discovery that bodily illness is the gate to the soul, and that the soul is the source of all true healing. A powerful read for those interested in the spirituality of the body and sickness as a spiritual journey."

—**Reginald A. Ray**, author of *Touching Enlightenment* and the CD series, *Your Breathing Body,* and spiritual director of Dharma Ocean Foundation

"Alison Anton has an amazing gift for clear communication with the spirit and the body. I was delighted by the depth of her insights while reading her **True Healing** book."

—**Jeffrey Allen**, intuition trainer and author of *Energy Mastery*

"Alison Anton's **True Healing** will set anyone who suffers with chronic symptoms on an inner path to lasting relief. This book incorporates meditation techniques and authentic examples from Alison's own life that help bring about the desired spiritual experience."

—**David Hoffmeister**, author of *Unwind Your Mind Back to God* and *Awakening through A Course In Miracles*

"**True Healing** is just that, a deep and realistic look at what it takes to heal. Alison Anton approaches healing from one of the most powerful places possible—having to overcome failure, illness and expectation. A must read for those of us who are not perfect!"

—**Lisa Wimberger**, author of *New Beliefs, New Brain* and *Neurosculpting: A Whole-Brain Approach to Heal Trauma, Rewrite Limiting Stories, and Find Wholeness*

TRUE HEALING

ALSO BY ALISON ANTON

Your Mind Is Your Medicine Audio Course

What Color Is Your Bubble?
Children's Tools for Intuition, Levels 1 and 2

TRUE HEALING

Spiritual Medicine for Every Illness

ALISON ANTON

ANTON GUILD
of Spiritual Medicine

Copyright © 2014 by **Alison Anton**

All rights reserved. No part of this publication may be reproduced, distributed or transmitted in any form or by any means, without prior written permission.

Anton Guild of Spiritual Medicine
PO Box 84
Niwot, CO 80544
AntonGuild.com

This book offers spiritual inspiration and meditation as a compliment to medical treatment. The author and publisher do not recommend use of the information to treat or diagnose disease, or as a substitute for advice from a qualified, licensed physician. It is advised that you consult with a licensed physician before making any changes to diet, medications, or exercise. Neither the publisher nor the author shall be liable for any physical, psychological, emotional, financial, or commercial damages, including, but not limited to, special, incidental, consequential, or other damages. Any references, materials, practices, products, or services are listed for spiritual inspiration only, for use when discussing your health with your doctor.

Design: Jackson D. Carson (jacksondcarson.com)

True Healing / Alison Anton. -- 1st ed.

ISBN 978-1491047743

CONTENTS

Do not ask Spirit to heal the body.
Ask rather that Spirit teach you the right
perception of the body.

~A COURSE IN MIRACLES

INTRODUCTION

I NEED A MIRACLE

I have a love-hate relationship with miracle healing stories. I love the way they open our minds and inspire us, the way they give us hope. The Bible tells the story of Jesus traveling through a large crowd. When a woman touched the fringe of his robe, she was miraculously healed without a conscious act by Jesus. He said to her: "Daughter, your faith has healed you. Be freed of your suffering."

Who suffering with chronic illness wouldn't want this? Who wouldn't want to heal simply through the power of faith and wishes?

Yet, when our wishes for healing don't come true, we often end up discouraged and spiritually defeated. Hoping for miracles is a seriously draining venture for a soul incarnated. Anyone suffering with illness wants a miracle, but unfortunately, we waste a lot of energy trying to have one.

In my early twenties, I was bitten by a tick and infected with a swarm of bacteria. The effect on my body is called Lyme Disease. My symptoms appeared slowly and progressively, but it wasn't until years later that the proverbial shit hit the fan. My husband and I separated, and at the same time, I stepped out of my role as a spiritual healer to focus on clinical nutrition. Bad move. My soul didn't appreciate so much focus on the body and so little on Spirit. It also hated being away from the best source of spiritual support I've had in this lifetime, my husband. My body couldn't handle the resulting stress, and my immune system flopped.

My body gave in to the infection, leaving me with two grueling years of all-over pain and rock bottom fatigue. I developed an assortment of autoimmune conditions, kidney disease, mold toxicity, and a dreadful jaw infection, requiring removal of two molars and re-opening all four wisdom tooth sockets so the decomposing mush could be scooped out like gelato. I became a tired, aching, and depressed me. I couldn't leave the bubble of my house for more than a couple hours without feeling totally exhausted or gravely ill on my return. I slept a lot, even on days when I didn't leave my home at all.

Certainly, I was primed for my own miracle story. And I had it all figured out.

My "master miracle plan" included meditating three to four hours every day. I used the right spiritual tools, I sat in the right postures, and I ran the right energies. After each meditation, I blessed all beings, big and small. I thought if I was dedicated enough, pushed hard enough, and made myself spiritual enough, I could cure my sickness. Not only would I be cured, I'd also be levitating.

But I'm also a realist—a "trust in God, but tie your horse up, too" kind of girl—so I made sure to cover all the bases. I visited a plethora of doctors and healers. I used Functional Medicine, German Medicine, acupuncturists, body workers, energy workers, hypnotherapy, and lots of yoga. I was doing my work, and I expected someone else to bend over backward to do theirs. Since I was paying them, weren't they just as responsible for getting me out of this mess as I was?

After six months, I hadn't improved at all. In fact, I was sicker. Not only were my physical symptoms heightened, I had also generated a sense of resistance and fear toward my illness. I resented my doctors for not being able to heal me. Even my meditation practice stressed me out. Just the thought of sitting with myself, again, made my nerves stand up like Einstein's hair. I was worse off than before. This sudden realization took me into the darkest corners of my mind. My nightmare had come true: I had failed.

I had been through one other such "dark night of the soul" at age twenty, when my childhood friend committed suicide. In both these spiritually raking episodes, I felt like I had been dropped into a deep hole, totally impossible to scale. I often wished the hole were made for my coffin. I couldn't find a reason to be here. The only thing I had left was the stark realization that I may never heal. I felt left out in the cold by God.

God never did come down from the clouds to wipe my slate clean. No one doctor and no one pill had the magic ingredient to cure me. There was no overnight revelation. I never saw a light in a tunnel. And dammit! I still can't levitate.

And I still don't have my "miracle" story. Yet, I can honestly say that I am not suffering.

My Iron Man Meditation Marathon didn't get me out of the struggle I was in. It wasn't a particular doctor or a revolutionary treatment, nor did my healing occur by "thinking myself well" with positive affirmations or prayer. Instead, the universe forced me into letting my illness be what it was. I simply began to develop a sense of neutrality, or equanimity, toward my symptoms. Instead of seeing my illness as something that was out to get me, or that made me a "lesser" spiritual being, I explored my symptoms and the areas in my body that were expressing them. Since I couldn't fight my illness, I allowed it.

As my mental and spiritual attitude shifted from expectation to allowance, my need for an easy, no-stress meditation grew. I needed something I could practice every day, something that didn't push me over the spiritual edge or take too much time or energy. I began to tie in the foundational elements from each of the three schools of spiritual thought I've been trained in this lifetime.

In 1995, at the age of twenty-four, I began a series of clairvoyant trainings as taught by the late Reverend Lewis Bostwick at his spiritual sanctuary, the Church of Divine Man, in Northern California. I became an ordained minister at a young age, but it wasn't until a few years later, in 1997, that I discovered my spiritual treasure chest, the universal curriculum from *A Course in*

Miracles, a manual and workbook that teaches forgiveness as the spiritual path. Fast forward several years, and I began to incorporate Buddhist embodied awareness practices into my spiritual repertoire.

Together, the tools and concepts from these three schools are the backbone of my spiritual life. They make up the elements of the five-step meditation outlined in this book, a practice that allows healing to penetrate into the mind of the soul, the only place where True Healing can really occur. The daily thirty-minute practice involves:

1. Anchoring the body to the earth
2. Scanning the four quadrants of the body for pain, symptoms, or intense emotion
3. Looking into a "hotspot" and deepening the body-scan
4. Seeing the pain as a call for love
5. Inviting Spirit to heal the perceived lack

As I deepened into the True Healing practice, my body became less and less of a machine that was failing me, and more and more of an organic, living container for Spirit. The more I explored this vessel, the more I saw Spirit flooding the empty open spaces between the pockets of pain. The openness, it turned out, took up far greater space than the density of my symptoms. I came to know first-hand that the river of Spirit never ceases to run, in sickness or in health (or even whether the body is alive or dead).

Through the practice of True Healing, I discovered that the body doesn't do the healing, food doesn't do the healing, exercise doesn't do the healing, medicine doesn't do the healing. Even healers don't do the healing. *Spirit* does the healing. All forms of healing that bring health to the physical body are secondary to the healing that has already occurred in the soul. As I recognized this, the less I punished my body for being sick and the happier and healthier I became.

It feels good not to have to worry about whether or not my body—or this food or this special procedure or this practice—will be able to "fix" me. Once I took the responsibility of healing away from the body and placed it back into the hands of Spirit, my body could finally reply to the concurrent healing that was happening on a deeper, foundational level.

I still need to maintain a watchful and mindful lifestyle. I'm far from perfect. Like all bodies, I need to eat well and exercise. I meditate daily, take supplements, and still visit doctors and healers of all kinds. But even my medical appointments have become more of a coming together of souls, a camaraderie of sorts, rather than a desperate attempt to force someone else to come up with my solutions.

A heavy weight has been lifted from my soul, and I can genuinely say that I am not suffering with illness. I have the energy to run my training programs and healing services, and to travel to lead workshops and retreats. I can eat out at many of my favorite restaurants and have an easier approach in how I care for my body, mind, and soul.

As they say in music, I'm good enough for jazz. And as anyone who is sick and suffering knows, that is a miracle.

TRUE HEALING

THE TEN PRINCIPLES OF TRUE HEALING

1. As the only aspect of the mind that has remained whole, Spirit is the only requisite for True Healing.

2. True Healing restores wholeness in the mind. It is not limited to mental and ego constructs like curing, fixing, or making a disease go away.

3. A soul suffers only because it severs itself from its source and sees itself as an autonomous, isolated identity.

4. True Healing happens at the level of the soul, where the origin of suffering resides.

5. Spirit lovingly underlies every experience, even pain, discomfort, and disease, but we have to look deep inside our circumstances to see it.

6. Health or disease in the body are not indications of how spiritually enlightened or unenlightened we are.

7. The body responds to the signals the mind believes—fear or love.

8. The present moment is where all True Healing takes place because it is the only moment where Spirit exists.

9. As humans, one of the best place to experience the present moment is through the physical body. For people who are sick, spiritual practice can be an embodied discipline.

10. Illness or any uncomfortable situation we face in life can be given a spiritual purpose and used as an opportunity rather than an obstacle for True Healing.

PART I

THE ORIGIN OF SUFFERING

CHAPTER 1

WHO SUFFERS?

Receiving a diagnosis of chronic or terminal illness is a life-altering, gut-wrenching test of the human soul. Life was hard enough when we were healthy, and now we have to cope with pain, fatigue, fear, resentment, loneliness... you fill in the blank.

Many spiritual teachings tell us that all bodies suffer. One look out the front window proves it: the kid next door just fell off her bike and broke her arm; the man walking by just got word that his wife is leaving him for someone else; the neighbor across the street can't start her car and she's late for her dream interview. A few blocks away, someone ran a red light, killing a mother of two small children. Whether we're sick or healthy, suffering is simply the human condition.

Or is it?

According to *A Course in Miracles*, the spiritual curriculum founded upon the practice of forgiveness, suffering is a perceived lack of wholeness in the mind. But the mind isn't "only human," as they say. The mind doesn't start in the body. From the perspective of the Course, the idea of suffering begins somewhere deep within the mind before the body was ever made.

For the purpose of this book, and to give you a framework for how suffering can be viewed from a spiritual perspective, let's say the idea of suffering started within the mind of the soul.

From a macrocosmic view, everything is contained within one, big Universal Mind. Some might call this greater mind, God, Goddess, Oneness, the Great Spirit, the Source, the Supreme Being, or the All. To use a title that isn't associated with a particular religion or gender, I'll use "Universal Mind" to refer to the all-encompassing mind in which everything is so intimately contained.

The Universal Mind is creative by nature. It creates, and it does so by extending or expanding itself. Yet it holds its creations, its thoughts, its ideas, and its intentions *within* itself. I like to think of all creation as a bubble of light that expands and radiates. As an idea within the Universal Mind, nothing ever leaves the expanding bubble of creation. For example, we could think of Spirit as a creative offshoot of the Universal Mind, and the soul as a creative offshoot of Spirit.

Let's think of these offshoots as the roots and branches of a big oak tree. Roots and branches extend from the trunk yet stay connected to their source. Since the Spirit and the soul are creative ideas within the Universal Mind, both are held together via an all-encompassing, life-supporting root system. As spiritual beings, we never leave our divine source.

But we can *think* we can. And here's where suffering actually begins.

Somewhere along the line—within the mind of the soul, let's say—we imagined ourselves as existing outside of our source. A branch broke off from the trunk and thought of itself as its own tree. A soul cannot actually sever from the mind of its creator, but since we think we did, we make believe it is so. As separated limbs, we see ourselves as set apart from the warmth and security, the oneness and connectedness, the love and adoration of Spirit.

A soul that thinks of itself as splintered from the taproot of Spirit cannot perceive of itself as whole. It views itself as incomplete and its environment as unsatisfactory. Without the fertile soil of the tree of life, the broken branch experiences isolation and fear. When the mind of the soul suffers like this, it projects its suffering outward, creating a false universe, an image based in fear.

Included in the soul's fear-based fabrication is a false interpretation of itself. This false interpretation includes the 3D form, the human body. The body and all physical form as we see it is a projection thrown outward from the soul, like images from a movie cast onto a big screen. Yet in reality, divine creation remains wholly connected at all times; nothing can be splintered into separate pieces. Since the idea of separation is projected out and away—versus extended from within—our physical form might not be the most authentic interpretation of who we truly are.

Herein lies the question: Can the body or anything in the world around it be the cause of suffering? If the body is a false idea within the mind of a soul that thinks of itself as separate from its divine origins, couldn't we say it's the soul that suffers first?

If we pull our experiences apart as we would a Russian nesting doll, we eventually come to our true cause of suffering: the soul's decision to see itself as separate from its source. Sickness is not the cause of suffering. A divorce is not the cause of suffering. Nor are accidents, deaths, faulty genetics, the flooded basement, or the barking dog next door. Cessation of suffering comes when the soul enkindles the memory of itself as a creative extension of the one Universal Mind, as a whole, complete, and perfect being.

There are so many aspects to the mind, from our highest selves all the way down into the body. All of us have awareness of ourselves in physical form: we feel pain, pleasure, and everything in between. We also know we think because we have ideas; we plan and comprehend. We also have spiritual or ethereal experiences in waking life or in dreams. We are multidimensional beings.

All the myriad aspects of the mind are like a big layer cake. At the base of the cake is the layer of Spirit. Spirit underlies all else, with the exception of the Universal Mind, the plate on which all creation rests. Spirit is the Divine Self, the direct creative extension of the Universal Mind.

For our purposes, we can call Spirit a "layer" or a "level," but in truth, Spirit cannot be separated into tiers, structures, or identities. It remains undivided from its source. Never having left its home within the shelter of the Universal Mind, Spirit has no need for healing because it has always remained whole. It has no need for learning because it already knows all.

From a Christian cosmology, we could think of Spirit as the "Son of God." Or, within the landscape of some Buddhist traditions, we could envision Prajñaparamita as the representation of Spirit. Prajñaparamita is a deity known as the "Great Mother of All Buddhas."

The second layer of the cake is the soul. The soul is an extension of Spirit, a wing of love. It is eternal and divine, just like its creator. Like Spirit, the soul is not made of 3D material; it is made of intention and light. The soul's true essence remains an integral part of the greater whole, bestowing upon the soul the opportunity to retain access to all the divine attributes of Spirit: holiness, freedom, creative license, limitless joy, eternal life, and the great rays of knowledge extended from all creation.

Yet, many souls are split off from full awareness of who they truly are. These detached souls identify with the third layer of the cake, the ego. The direct result of separation from Spirit, the ego is the soul's inclination to make itself into a separate "I" or "me." It is the exact opposite of Spirit. If Spirit is wholeness and oneness with all, the ego is separateness and autonomy from all.

Since the Universal Mind didn't create us to be separate from it and all of creation, the ego can be seen as a false perception within the mind of the soul—a bug in the program, so to speak—that leads the soul to perceive itself as a separate entity outside of the big expanding bubble of creation.

The ego poses a big problem for the soul. In its attempts to be successful as a detached entity, the ego doesn't allow the soul to remember itself as an extension of the divine. *In no case can the soul actually get sick or die.* Yet the ego convinces the soul that it is mortal, predisposed to the cycles of birth, illness, karma, and death.

We could simply call this separation a mistake. There's no sin involved; there's nothing we did to deserve punishment or retribution. The soul simply took a wrong turn somewhere. Fortunately for us, all errors in the mind can be corrected, and all wrong turns can be righted.

At the very top of our "mind cake" is the mass of muscles, bones, water, nerves, minerals, and all the stuff that makes up the physical body.

Contrary to popular belief, you are not your body. Instead of a mind that is inside your body—like the brain or nervous system—your body is inside your mind. Your soul thinks of itself as a body with structural boundaries. That thought is projected out from the mind of the soul, creating a body in 3D form.

The body is always expressing what the soul thinks, how the soul perceives itself. It is a window into the soul. Instead of a curse or a hindrance on our path—which it might seem to be sometimes—the body holds tremendous value for us. Rather than bypassing, discarding, or transcending the physical body, we can use it as a road map. By paying close attention to it, the body affords us an opportunity for True Healing. The more we inhabit the body (in sickness or in health), the more we see it as a divine temple for Spirit. With practice, awareness of the body leads to the eventual cessation of suffering.

Cessation of suffering is True Healing. It is the divine nectar of love that seeps up from our higher selves as Spirit and soaks through all the layers of the cake to correct our misperceptions about who we are and what it means to be truly healed.

True Healing restores to wholeness, realigning the soul to its original state as a divine expression of Spirit. Attempts to cure or fix the myriad forms of suffering in the body (illness, pain, symptoms) without addressing the one and only cause of suffering at the soul level lack this final, consummate ingredient.

CHAPTER 2

A DISEASE OF THE SOUL

Remember those marble runs we had when we were kids? A marble starts at the top, riding through corkscrew slides and tracks, passing through turns and twists, making its way through various hoops, spinny-tunnels, and bumpers along the way. Eventually, the marble lands in the little cup at the end.

The cup at the end is your body. Your progression through the marble run is the process of karma, or the cascading law of cause and effect. If you have a perception about something at the top, inevitable outcomes are bound to occur at the bottom. You can think of the marble run, or the progression of karma, as the "if this, then that" effect. If "this" happens at the top, then "that" happens at the bottom.

The marble run always starts with Spirit. Spirit sends the original signal, or marble, down the run. The top of the run could be thought of as the Kingdom of Heaven or the original dwelling place created by the Universal Mind. This is the state of being in which we experience utter peace, the "oneness" of the universe. It is our true and original nature. It is where we all come from.

Spirit is so close to the Universal Mind that it only relays exactly what the Universal Mind would relay. It relays love. Since Spirit remains completely intact with its source, it speaks what it hears from its source. It naturally extends love. Let's think of the voice of Spirit as a big white marble with the word "Love" etched into it.

Next in line along the marble run is the soul. The soul is the extension of Spirit. As the love-etched marble rolls from Spirit to the soul, it brings with it all the divine attributes from Heaven. It bestows the soul with eternal life and all the things that go with it. These are peace, safety, security, love, light, and complete well-being, to name just a few.

But there's a caveat: the soul has to hear the right voice. It has to *listen* to Spirit to know it *is*

Spirit. And if it's not listening, the soul can be dissuaded.

Enter stage left, the ego.

Somewhere along the marble run, the love-etched marble rolled through a puddle of grease, tainted by doubt. By the time the smudged marble reached the soul, the soul not only picked up on Spirit's original signal of love, but it also got an inkling of uncertainty. The soul got smeared with the grease. Even though this uncertainty was a mere blemish on the beautiful white marble, the soul just couldn't shake it: "Which signal is real?" it thought. "Is love real or is doubt real? And if doubt is real, then who the heck am I?" Perfectly cast for the part, the ego's first line on the script reads, "Who *am* I?"

With its identity in question, fear began to permeate the mind of the soul.

Herein lies the origination of the mistake. Having doubt isn't a sin; it's just a thought or a question. The correct answer was there all along—and still is—etched forever into the beautiful white marble. "You are Love", answers Spirit.

Yet fear leaves the soul deaf and blind. The soul does not hear. And as the marble rolls along, the soul becomes more and more identified with the splotch of grease. The fear doubles, then triples, and then multiplies exponentially. Around and around it goes, deeper and deeper into a never-ending spiraling tunnel, creating all kinds of concepts, theories, and cosmologies along the way, hoping to come up with a clear definition of itself within the universe around it.

This new definition of itself does not include Spirit. The soul is now deathly afraid of its true nature—of being intimately joined with all creation—and afraid it will lose the only identity it remembers, the ego.

As soon as the soul started to follow fear-based conversations, it left the wholeness of Spirit behind and chose separation, incompletion, and autonomy instead. It chose to be broken rather than whole.

If the soul identifies with the ego—if it listens to the little splotch of grease on the marble instead of the marble itself—the soul may project outward an image of itself as a separate, isolated entity. It wants to be its own marble. What better way to make an idea real than with a real-life material substance? Via the projection of an idea about itself, the ego solidifies a body in physical form.

THE DISAPPEARANCE OF THE BODY

Like everything that manifests on the physical plane, it begins with a perception. Perception is always based on what we believe about the universe, the world, ourselves, someone else, or any circumstance in our lives.

We carry our perceptions with us wherever we go like a Northwesterner carries an umbrella. Except instead of taking the umbrella out *when* it rains, we take it out *before* it rains. And then we ask the sky to rain on us so we have a good reason for carrying the umbrella around all the time. The rain makes our perception real so we can say, "See? I *knew* it would rain!"

The ego, too, created something to make itself real so it could say, "See? I *knew* I was real!"

That "something" is the body.

Gary Renard, in his book, *The Disappearance of the Universe,* recounts several conversations with his two ascended teachers who propose that the entire physical universe is an illusion made in our minds. This concept is widely recognized in many of the world's spiritual traditions and is one of the founding principles of *A Course in Miracles*. It is taught that we should take notice of what we perceive, and that just because we believe what we see doesn't necessarily make it true.

Dr. Wayne Dyer says that believing is seeing. It's not the other way around. What we perceive is very real to us only because we *believe* it is there. The body and everything that comes with it—like pain, illness, and death—seem very real, but only because we believe in the idea of physicality, space, time, shape, and form. This is the perception of the ego. If we believe in the ego, we believe in separation. In turn we'll see our mind as separate from the oneness of the greater Universal Mind. We'll perceive the mind as inside the body, rather than the body as inside the mind. In other words, we envision a physical body in the efforts to try to encase a mind that is afraid to be a part of the Universal Whole.

Suffering in the body starts in the mind of the soul. Anything that has chiseled itself into an individualized, separated identity does not perceive itself an integrated element within the one Universal Mind. It does not see itself as whole. Anything that is not whole has not healed. From this perspective—whether the body is sick or healthy by the standards of our culture—the separated soul has a very serious illness: It is picking up on the ego's signals and listening to them.

True Healing comes when we believe something very different about ourselves; we remember ourselves as Spirit. In this process of spiritual resurrection, Spirit becomes more and more real to us. And eventually a tipping point is reached when we identify more with Spirit than we do with the body. With a new belief system in place, the old view disappears (literally) and a whole new world arises, just as if we were coming out of a dream.

If you're reading this book, you're very likely on a path to enlightenment via the physical form. You are unwinding your way out of the ego's fear-based perception and back into the Spirit's love-based perception.

Thankfully, your body can be used to your advantage in this process. At every moment, the body tells you exactly who and what you're listening to. Are you listening to the fear signals of the ego? With careful attention, you can learn to hear another signal.

CHAPTER 3

THE BODY RESPONDS

A few years ago, I had a lucid dream in which I was sitting in the cockpit of a spacecraft that responded to my mind. I simply put my foot on the pedal, and once it recognized my foot, a kind of connectivity happened between my mind and the ship. I could fly wherever I wanted, no radar or flight equipment needed. As soon as I had a thought or a vision of where I wanted to go, the ship would fulfill the order. I felt so personally connected to the ship that, in a very kinesthetic sense, I could say that the ship and I were "of one mind."

Not too long after my dream, my husband and I went to the IMAX Theater in Denver to see the movie *Avatar* in 3D. There's a harried and emotional scene where Jake, the hero of our story, was required to fly a large, wild, dinosaur-like bird. But first, he had to create a psychic, interpersonal connection with it. Once the connection was established, the bird could be commanded with Jake's mind.

Needless to say, once saddled up and ready to go, Jake realized pretty quickly that he needed to get his act together—like yesterday—if he actually wanted to commandeer this "ship." He was on a kamikaze run, and since he was holding the reins with his thoughts, he only had a few seconds to get his mind clear, his body grounded, and his signals uncrossed before crashing into the side of the cliff or being catapulted to the depths below.

Thankfully, any of the ensuing PTSD from the bird's erratic dive-bombing, fishtailing, jerks, twists, and somersaults was allayed with this simple recognition: When Jake became clear in *his* mind, the bird became clear in *its* mind. From then on, the two communicated beautifully on their in-flight adventures and psychic joy rides.

I had goose bumps watching this scene. I realized my body was the ship, and I had a precious resource that could help me move through my separation as a soul and bring me toward True Healing. The imagery helped me see that the physical body is a biological vehicle that simply responds to the impulses of something higher, the soul.

Just as an antenna picks up on all kinds of radio waves, the body picks up on all kinds of signals. When we tune a radio to listen to our favorite music or program, we set it to the right station. The same is true of the body. We tune our bodies to pick up on specific signals that we've learned to respond most readily to. From the body's perspective, it's all about responding correctly and efficiently to the signals it gets.

In a sense, the body is an organic, biological vehicle that responds directly and intimately to its environment from the top down. If the soul believes the fear signals it hears from the ego, the body responds to those signals.

Fear signals are sent through the body in a series of reactions. They start in the brain and travel to every single cell in the body. The cells then respond to the signals by initiating a biological reaction—a behavior—appropriate to the signals they receive. Fear signals become quite obvious when we experience them on the physical plane. They translate into pain, heated emotion, intense feelings, obsessive desires, disturbed thoughts, or surges of energy.

Thankfully, our job isn't to make fear reactions go away. That's like trying to empty the ocean with a teacup. On the contrary, we learn to pay close attention to these reactions. The more aware we are of the body and how it responds to its environment, the more clearly we see how our reactions affect our health.

In paying attention to our bodies, we might see that, when there's fear (in the form of pain, nagging symptoms, or the welling of emotion) the natural tendency of the ego is to react with more fear. In other words, fear creates fear. We get caught in a vicious, seemingly endless cycle. This is "survival mode." Survival mode is an over-inflated tendency in the body to react to fear with fear. In survival mode, stress creates more stress. Soon it becomes a gargantuan snowball rolling down a very long hill.

In a healthy state, the survival mechanism in the body turns on and off quickly and efficiently. For instance, when we step out into the street and a truck comes zooming by, the body naturally jerks out of the way without thinking about it. After the startling event, the body brings itself back into homeostasis within a few seconds or minutes. But when the survival switch gets stuck on, it takes longer and longer to self-regulate.

There's a story of a Zen monk who went to his teacher and asked, "How much ego should I have in this world?" The teacher replied, "Just enough so you don't get hit by a truck crossing the street." We all need the ego to survive in a physical body. But too much ego in the body—too much fear—leads to a chronic, debilitating cascade of physiologic reactions that perpetuate ill health or disease. In survival mode, the body goes into a fear response that won't turn off. For those of us stuck in survival mode, the simple task of walking into the grocery store may feel like we are stepping out into roaring traffic.

An overly fearful survival response occurs when the body is stuck in high gear, reacting to everything as if it were always going to get hit by a truck. In these cases, the body has a very hard time coming back into a restorative, regenerative, homeostatic state. It responds to everyday stressors as though they were life or death situations.

Survival mode raids the body's storehouse of energy so we can "put up our dukes" or "run for our lives." Being in survival actually takes a tremendous amount of energy. It's hard work, and there's little time or energy for anything else. A body in motion tends to stay in motion; once a fear pattern starts to etch a pathway through the mind, it digs itself deeper and deeper into the body.

Here's an anecdote to describe this cascading fear process: Mary falls ill and has some pain associated with the illness. She gets a little scared of the pain, but shakes it off and moves on. We could think of Mary as having taken a stick and written the word "fear" into a pool of water. As she writes the word, she gets a glimpse of the letters, but before she blinks, they're gone. This is a normal, acute survival response. It's the ability to self-regulate under stress.

But let's say Mary's pain continues. It hasn't gone away in weeks. She then becomes fearful of the fact that she's been feeling the pain for so long. She is afraid she might be chronically ill. The fear leaves her restless and nervous. This time, Mary writes her fear into sand. Although the wind or waves will soon cover the graffiti, the words are perfectly legible for a little while.

Mary's pain continues, and her fear continues as well. Her body now associates her pain with fear, and the memory of fear brings on more fear. Mary panics. She envisions her future as severe and painful. The fear etches itself into her body and mind. Now Mary carves her fear into stone.

Mary desperately needs to train her mind to listen to a new signal. She sees where the marble rolls when she listens to fear. Now it's time to see where it rolls when she listens to love, the signal of Spirit.

With practice, Mary may find that Spirit is always present under her fear, no matter how loud, domineering, or convincing her fear may be. Remember that the communication of Spirit (the pure white marble) always comes first. It underlies everything. That's why True Healing is available for us in *every* situation, even in our darkest hours. Spirit is there under the body's reactions and interpretations. And where Spirit is, healing is.

CHAPTER 4

MOVING INTO THRIVAL

There are so many layers to fear. The body—originally as a manifestation of the ego—is a reflection of fear. But like Jake in *Avatar* riding the wild bird, when the mind of the soul changes what impulses it chooses to see and believe, the body responds. The more we listen to Spirit under everything that happens, the body becomes less and less fearful. This is what I call being in "thrival mode."

Thrival is our ability to be here in these bodies with less fear and more love. It's an expression of our Spirit-Nature made manifest on the physical plane. It's where we realistically look upon our situation and say, "Yes, I have an ego. Yes, I made a wrong turn somewhere. But I am Spirit, and my mistakes can be corrected."

Thankfully, we can use our illness and symptoms as an opportunity to make those corrections. By simply listening to our experiences—however painful they may be—the corrections are made.

In its most advanced form, thrival mode is the ability to trust our path no matter what is showing up in the here and now. That includes trusting illness and pain as the spiritual path, at least for the time being. Trusting illness as a spiritual journey is a hard concept to swallow at first. It goes against our very instinct. Instinct says that pain and illness are things to fear and loathe. But if illness has shown up, I guarantee there's something else there, something that's calling us to turn and look.

This calling is our intuition.

Spiritual work requires intuition, not instinct. While instinct convinces us to *run* for our lives from scary and painful events, intuition urges us to *look* for our lives. It gently asks us to turn toward these things when they occur, to hold firm, and to look on with presence. Jesus said, "Stand uprightly" and proposed that we shine the light of Spirit onto our fears and demons.

As we get more and more comfortable facing fear or pain or illness, the body learns to access a whole new dimension of being. This is the intuitive side of the body that sees a clear, bird's-eye view. Intuition corrects our perspective; it allows us to not only see the body and mind as sick, but also as whole. We can't see our wholeness if we resist or run from the things we think can sabotage our well-being. As Spirit, nothing can sabotage our well-being since well-being *is* the state of Spirit. Turning away or shrinking in fear's presence is the very act that keeps the separation of the soul in place.

Intuition is not the ability to see what may be lurking behind the shadows so that we can fight it, kill it, or run from it. That's instinct. Intuition is the courage to look into the shadows and call upon the innate intelligence of Spirit to make corrections to our false perceptions about what we think is there. Intuition shows us that what's false is the notion that anything can hurt us in the first place.

Gandhi made a profound statement: "No one can hurt me without my permission." Ponder this for a minute. He was not saying that the body cannot be physically or emotionally hurt. Certainly, we all know that it can. He was saying that when it does, we have agreed to *see* it that way; we've given ourselves "permission" to get hurt.

To use his statement in the context of his own life, Gandhi was faced with a golden spiritual opportunity: He could see his assassin as a friend or he could see him as a foe. If he saw his assassin as a foe, he is indeed hurt. If he saw him as a friend, he is not. In either case, Gandhi's body is dead and gone, but his mind is freed only in the latter case.

What's in the shadow of our illness is just the ego, a part of our own mind that we think we've given permission to harm us. Yet it is just a shadow figure in the dark. The more we allow Spirit to be the engine for our bodies—and love, the fuel—the more courage we have to look toward the shadow and shine the light of Spirit upon it. And what we thought was there changes in front of our eyes. Nothing is foe in the eyes of Spirit.

When we set the intention to move into an intuitive space, the body progressively learns to become less reactive to its symptoms. It learns to stop the survival-based fear cycle before it goes bowling down the hill. Sure, symptoms might still be there, but the body is less and less caught up in them and less fear is generated around them. We start to see the symptoms for what they are now, not for what they might become later.

Thrival mode and intuition are like the checks-and-balances for the fear response. They go together like peas and carrots. When we're in the intuitive thrival mode—versus the instinctive survival mode—we could be faced with a stressful or fearful situation, yet manage the experience wisely. Uncomfortable experiences themselves don't go away (that's just life) but we don't generate as much fear toward them. This calms the nervous system and takes the body out of survival. From here, the body uses its needed energy to repair any damaged, tight, tender, or frozen areas that still hold fear. Ironically, instead of fear generating more fear, fear generates healing.

A CALL FOR LOVE

Spiritually speaking, there is no such thing as fear. Fear does not exist in the Kingdom of Heaven. It is a mammoth, overblown reaction made within the mind of the soul in response to a simple, innocent inkling of uncertainty. Instead of perceiving fear as it appears at face value, we can train ourselves to look at it a little differently.

A Course in Miracles suggests that there are merely two kinds of love. The first kind of love is the pure, eternal, true love extended from the Universal Mind to the heart of all creation. The second kind of love is a *call for love* in the temporary forms of fear, doubt, and pain. Fear is simply a call for love, a shout-out from the soul that it needs help.

Instinct and ego react to fear with fear. But intuition and Spirit react to fear with love. And they do so because they see fear for what it really is: a call for love.

When we see fear as a call for love, we give Spirit permission to enter and heal. A call for love is a call for healing. As Spirit enters the mind, it heals us at the core. It softens what was once hard, warms what was once frozen, and tickles what was once so serious. It heals the separation and soothes the ailing soul.

And the body responds.

PART II

STEPPING ONTO THE RED CARPET

CHAPTER 5

THE KARMA OF DISEASE

Every moment shows us the karmic expression, the cause and effect, of our life. The way we thought and acted in one moment paved the way for our thoughts and actions right now. Likewise, our thoughts and actions right now pave way for our future. In either case, the present moment is a fortuitous look at our footprint, where we came from and also where we are going.

Karma is similar to a frog jumping from one lily pad to the next. The circumstances it faces on top of its lily pad causes the frog to hop in a certain direction. Where the frog hops, where it lands, is the effect. Similarly, your reaction to your illness or current symptoms creates your future lily pad, your future now.

Your body in the present moment is your lily pad. Each moment you step fully into your experience on your lily pad, you have the opportunity to stop, look, and listen to your body and to the sensations, emotions, and reactions it's producing.

Sometimes we react with fear, panic, regret, or hatred to what's with us on our lily pad (when there's a flare-up of symptoms, when we don't get the results we want, when there's a lack of flies, a divorce, an encounter with an alligator, a blown tire, or faulty genetics). If we don't like how the body feels, it's natural to want to move away from that feeling, or the person, place, or thing we think caused our discomfort. Reactions like these are instinctual. It's the ego reacting to fear with fear, rather than responding to fear with love.

Thankfully, we don't need to resist or fight our reactions. While we're in this physical form, the body is going to react; that's what it does. It responds to the messages it hears. When we work with karma and the body in a conscious way, we don't attempt to change our reactions or to make them go away. All we need to do is become aware of them. Here, in the present moment on our lily pad, knowledge is our greatest power. When we are aware, we shine the light of truth on our circumstances. I had a teacher once who said that spiritual work is 99 percent awareness and one percent action. There's not a whole lot to do. With simple awareness, Spirit takes over and True Healing happens.

Simply staying present with the body and its (often uncomfortable) expressions of karma feels like sharing a problem with a good friend. Even if our friend offers us little advice or emotional comfort, sharing our experiences heals us. It may be scary to articulate at first, but just by sharing, just by saying something allows the space for healing. Something moves, something changes, something releases.

The body responds this way, too. When we bring our undivided attention to the body, it tells its stories as it sees them. These stories are our karma. Once told, the karma arises, releases, and passes away bit by bit. As the karma arises and passes, space opens up in the body and freedom emerges in the soul. The longer and harder we close our ears to the stories reflected in our bodies, the less space our karma has to free itself.

The body is always eager to communicate, whether it's sick, healthy, or somewhere in between. We have the perfect opportunity in this lifetime—and with this illness—to finally listen. When we don't listen, when we don't fully greet our reactions and experiences, they end up trapped in the muscles. They build up in the tissues, pile onto the organs, and fill up the subatomic particles in the energy field. We store them deep in the mind, deep in soul, and deep in the body.

All these stored experiences eventually need to be released. If we're unconscious to the stockpile of karma in the physical and etheric bodies, it unconsciously seeps out. This karmic ooze expresses itself in often painful or uncomfortable ways.

When I was seventeen, my close childhood friend, Laura, suffered through an attempt at cutting one of her wrists with a serrated knife. She was nowhere near successful and was safe from immediate harm, but was in obvious emotional, mental, and spiritual turmoil. After spending several hours with her at her apartment, she made me promise not tell anyone about what happened.

I went into a total freeze. This was a big deal, but as a teenager with such little life experience, I didn't know what to do. At the same time, "freeze" wasn't in my vocabulary. It was never in my survival makeup. My natural instinct was, and still is, one of action. It was never like me to hold my tongue; I often said or did things that disturbed people in one way or another because I thought it was the right thing to do. It's hard for me to believe that I let a promise—albeit to one of my best friends—keep me from taking action under such serious circumstances.

But I kept my promise and did nothing. I froze the experience deep in my mind. Laura and I never spoke of it again, nor did I tell another soul.

Four years later, Laura's body was found in the mountains of Big Sur, California. She and a friend rigged the exhaust pipe into their car and committed a double suicide.

At the time of writing this book, Laura's death was over twenty years ago, but the trauma still lurks within my body and mind.

One of the myriad ways the karma from this traumatic event has shown up for me is through my spiritual teaching and counseling. For many years, a tremendous amount of nervous, resistant energy (often terror) would arise when students or clients went into their emotional and spiritual dark nights. The resistance came in as an intense pulling sensation in my solar plexus that was often accompanied by a stabbing pain deep in my gut. My awareness would leave my body and a white haze would flood my energy field, similar to the feeling right before fainting.

If a client was in deep spiritual turmoil, I froze. I got as far away as I could and pretended I didn't see. I even quit my healing practice (more than once) just so I wouldn't have to help people through such dark and difficult times. If I couldn't see, I couldn't help. If I couldn't help, I wasn't responsible. If I wasn't responsible, I wasn't guilty. I shut the door and said, "I don't see."

The irony is that I'm a clairvoyant healer. Clairvoyance means "clear-seeing." I also teach other people how to see. Lugging around the "I don't see" picture caused ill health in my body and was a grave disservice to the struggling people who were called to work with me. Only by allowing this unconscious karma to come to the surface—rather than stuffing it away or running from it—was I able to move through it. It still isn't easy, but whenever a layer of this particular karma arises in my body, it's more benign. It's easier for me to hold firm to my true vibration. It doesn't pull me away from my path.

Some Buddhists believe in an unconscious part of the mind that stores unprocessed experiences; the alaya-vijnana or "storehouse consciousness." It's like a backpack we carry with us on the walkabout of the soul. If we do not willingly open the backpack in this lifetime, allowing the contents some space to breathe, we take them with us into the next life. Our untold stories remain forever in the backpack, peeking out every once in a while like little gremlins until we are ready to really listen. Our karma plays out again and again. It keeps us hopping unconsciously from one lily pad to the next.

Our karma shows up in many ways. Karma sometimes feels good and karma sometimes feels bad. In either case, as soon as we become aware of it, karma naturally dissolves itself little by little. The soul's course starts to shift. But we have to be willing to greet our karma when it shows up, however painful or unpleasant it may be. Otherwise, we're putting the book back on the shelf, only for it to be pulled out and dusted off at some future date.

We can learn to allow karma to settle. But life on this golden pond is never perfect. Like the sun rising and setting, we have to expect the up-and-down forces of karma to play out in our lives. As long as we're in these bodies, "karma happens." Karma will arise and pass, arise and pass, arise and pass.

We must stand up and greet karma as it is. We are ready to look at whatever arises, including pain, anger, depression, or anything else surfacing around illness. It's only the ego that doesn't want us to see. Part of the ego's plan to keep us in the dark is to hold us back from fully experiencing our lily pads, our bodies, in the present moment. It keeps us unconscious, or unaware. It puts us on autopilot and we hop from one lily pad to the next. Then we wonder, "How on Earth did I get *here*?"

We all have karma. We're all working through fear-based energy and learning how to come out of the ego's thought system and back into Spirit's. This process can be long and arduous and can take many, many lifetimes. It takes many lifetimes just to recognize the importance of this process, and then many more to put it into action and make the intention real.

Karma usually dissolves in layers, like peeling the layers of an onion. Piece by piece, layer by layer, karma comes up to be resolved. We work the layers during the course of our lifetimes, and some layers remain dormant until we're ready for them to resolve. These layers might not show themselves in this lifetime.

This is why we can't compare our situation with anybody else's. If a specific quality of our karma has arisen that has resulted in illness or pain and we're pitting ourselves against the people around us who seem perfectly normal, perfectly happy, and perfectly perfect, we're not seeing the whole picture. We don't know what kind of karma they've moved through in past lives, or what will come up for them later this life, or in a future one.

Everyone has made a mistake that has resulted in tremendous karma: we've separated ourselves from Spirit. We're all in this game, but we're learning how to come out of it. Let's allow ourselves to have our karma come up, and forgive ourselves and others for anything that has impaired the process. When we muster the courage to stay with the body and our karma long enough to take a closer look at it, we will find Spirit under the initial anxiety or fear. And where there is Spirit, there is always healing.

CHAPTER 6

THE MIRACLE OF AWARENESS

I remember the first time I experienced a full-body energetic, psychic, and spiritual expression of my karma arising and passing from my body. I was in a long, silent Vipassana meditation retreat, practicing one of the Buddha's techniques of staying present with the body in a neutral, non-judgmental way. The instruction was simple: Move awareness from body part to body part, witnessing any sensations with equanimity, whether the sensations were gross or subtle, painful or pleasurable.

I followed the instructions to a tee, sweeping through my body slowly but continuously, trying not to give credence to any good feelings, pleasurable sensations, or happy thoughts, to those I deemed as bad, painful, or "unenlightened." As I delved deeper and deeper into meditating with my body, I noticed each location had its own distinct physical sensation. Every inch of my body expressed itself through sensation: heat, cold, tingling, numbing, pressure, pulling, blocking, flowing, strain, pain, tension, itchiness, dryness, dampness, heaviness, lightness. Even my earlobes, eyeballs, pinky toes, and fingernails expressed sensations!

Each area triggered an emotional expression, too, not just a physical one. Certain parts activated more fear, or resistance, loneliness, abandonment, or resentment in me than others. Other areas offered up a sense of tranquility, delight, humor, or creativity. Others were neutral. My awareness of body sensation became both physical and emotional. And pretty soon, my inner sensing became more and more acute, and I was able to pick up on very fine waves of subtle energy.

I have extensive training in clairvoyance. Clairvoyance is the ability to see energy, mental imagery, and non-corporeal, multidimensional things, such as the energetic and emotional fabric of the body, past and future lives, and light-beings without physical form. Once I engaged my clairvoyance in this body-based meditative setting, my karmic exploration took off. As I scanned my body from head to toe, I not only was able to feel the sensations in my body, I could *watch* them.

I watched and watched and watched. And I was in awe.

As the sensations swelled and receded, various scenes arose and fell away in my mind. Each scene was synchronous with the body part I was witnessing, consonant with the sensations. I remember my jaw nearly dropping as I swept through my left arm. Each section held layer upon layer of stored karmic experience ranging from this lifetime all the way back to thousands of years ago. I saw my limp, dead body hanging by the neck from the window of a castle wall in medieval Europe; I saw my body lying on a chaise lounge in the 1910's, crashed out on opium while my toddler son drowned in the swimming pool; I saw my friend and I walking up to a Roman government building not too long after Jesus' crucifixion.

And that was just my left arm!

Most of the experiences I witnessed held deep-seated emotional pain and often excruciating physical sensation as I watched the karma arise and pass from my body. There were many times I wished I could pack myself up and walk (um, more like, run) out of the meditation hall.

But I stayed there with my body and with my karma, as unwaveringly as I could, and allowed the stored experience to pass. A valve opened and the pain released. I didn't have to do anything but witness without judgment. I discovered that tapping into the body for spiritual healing is not a mental process or an analysis of thoughts or emotions. It's a present-time somatic witnessing of experiences as they show up "in the now" of the body.

As I watched the karma go, I felt the emotions shift and the pain dissolve. What I thought was so solid vanished in the blink of an eye. In these times of release, the cosmos inside my body literally opened up for me. I saw the universe within me, and I got to behold the spaciousness of myself as Spirit. The body, in my experience, very literally dissolved. There was absolutely no pain anywhere. There was nothing solid at all, nothing but an expansive sensation of love, the signal of Spirit. Under all the chaos and trauma of the ego was a pure and simple state of spiritual beingness: no turmoil, no drama, no karma, nothing generating, nothing perpetuating, just me being.

If I hadn't given myself the space to look, if I had walked out of the meditation hall every time I saw or experienced something uncomfortable or painful, all I would have taken from the process was the pain. Unbeknownst to me, the pain I stored from these experiences was popping up in my life at seemingly random times, via seemingly indiscriminate events. Like opening Pandora's Box, my karma was creating unconscious fear, anxiety, stress, and the feeling of incompletion. It would continue to do so until I could meet it with my neutral, non-judgmental awareness.

Staying present with my body through the discomfort was like taking myself lovingly by the hand and courageously walking through a dark, misty veil. I walked through the fear. I passed through the signals of the ego and into a space where I could once again hear Spirit calling me. I no longer felt that the Voice of Spirit hailed me from the edge of a deep chasm or through a dense, muffled forest. Spirit was so clear, so present, so strong, there was no way I could have missed it, even if I was deaf or blind.

The ability to witness the body and the signals it receives is an attribute of awareness. For instance, right now, notice the strain around your eyes as you focus to read these words. Were you even aware of the strain before you brought your attention there? Probably not. Every part of your body is expressing itself through a sensation right now, and you're likely not even aware of it, unless there's acute or prolonged pain, tension, or other aggravating symptoms.

Being able to notice the body and its sensations is embodied awareness. Your aware-self is the conscious part of you that is able to get into your body and observe how it responds. Through simple awareness, you become cognizant of the space inside you. Awareness is the red dot on the map that says, "You are here."

Awareness is like the icing on a cake, spread on top and in between the layers of the soul, the ego, and the body. Awareness can be spread wherever we choose for it to go. Since we can bring it to any and all parts of our mind, it can be used to consciously observe our experiences and reactions. There's nothing tricky or complex about it. It is simply the ability to witness.

Using awareness, we can bring attention to wherever we're holding tension in the physical body, as well as to the gross emotions, reactions, and strong waves of energy it emits. And when we get really good at it, our awareness gets keener and keener. It starts to sense the body's more subtle responses, such as feelings and energy, and ultimately, the pure, abiding presence of Spirit.

Simply because it observes the situation when it's called upon to do so, our awareness has tremendous capacity to initiate healing. It can't *do* the healing—Spirit does that—but it helps bring us there. It helps us get through the veil of illusion, or ego. With the ability of observation, we have the power to bring the soul into the present moment. Being in the present moment is spiritually important because, as Spirit, there is no other time or place that we are.

Spirit resides in the present moment. Spirit has no concept of past and future, and hence, no concept of time. If there's no past and no future, all that exists is the present. We won't be able to find Spirit in any other place but the present. Like a book that is constantly being turned to the current page, Spirit stays with "what is" right now. In fact, only "what is" *is* now.

As humans, experiencing our bodies in the present moment is the best way I know to begin the process of witnessing Spirit. Being in the body, observing the expressions and reflections of karma, gives us the perfect opportunity to see the situation as it is, and gives space for our karmic patterns to arise and pass naturally and with grace.

Spirit never asks us to sugar coat how we think or to dress up all pretty in order to get through the gates of Heaven. It just asks us to be honest. It requires us to see the truth of the situation. The truth is that we've been listening to fear, storing it, and replaying the old stories over and over.

These stories are not the truest expression of who we are as Spirit. Nonetheless, they are our organic experiences as souls. Acknowledging them is the first step on our path to True Healing.

CHAPTER 7

YOUR RED CARPET

Imagine you're a movie star stepping out of a limousine. Your driver courteously opens the door and helps you out of the warm safety of your chariot. As you step out, you are barraged with an immediate surge of energy: the shouts, whistles, and sneers from a huge crowd of fans, gawkers, critics, and paparazzi. The force of it nearly blows you away, and every cell in your body wants to cower back into your wheeled cave so you can be transported far, far away.

Then you realize you are on your Red Carpet, a long, empty strip of red lined by a golden balustrade. The crowd roars on either side, but right down the middle is a channel divinely laid out in front of you. You realize the carpet is just for you, and all you have to do is find the courage to stand uprightly and walk. You take a breath and go.

All around you, people shout words of adoration and encouragement, as well as insults and slander. The flashing of cameras nearly blinds you. People hold out their hands as you walk by, asking for your autograph or a touch of your hand. Roses and rotten tomatoes whoosh by your face, so close that you can feel the breeze on your cheeks as they fly by.

Inside your body, your nerves dance and your emotions reel. Partly frightened, partly excited, partly curious, and partly irritated, your body is a fleeting whirlwind of sensation. You notice everything around you and within you. And you keep walking.

Thank God for your Red Carpet. The Red Carpet is your center-line, your middle way, the axis that enables you to stay present and to witness what's going on within and without, whether you like what you're experiencing or not.

The Red Carpet is a space or an intention in your mind. It's your ability to allow. Your Red Carpet allows you to stay present inside your body, even in the midst of chaos, confusion, emotion, pain, scrutiny, or disarray.

On your Red Carpet, you realize how much space you have. There's plenty of room between you and the hoards of people on the other side of the rails. There's space between their opinions of you, your opinions of them, and your own opinions of yourself. On your Red Carpet, you don't need to change anything; you can allow everything that shows itself to you and still walk steadily on your path to True Healing.

In choosing the ego, we as souls separated from the taproot of Spirit. Unfortunately, there's no one else to blame. No one "did it" to us. As an offshoot of the Mind of Spirit, we are free beings with access to choose whatever, do whatever, and be however we want to be. Even though Spirit views the ego as a lie, or an erroneous perception in our minds, Spirit would never place restrictions on our freedom to *think* it's true, whether what we believe is the truth or not.

It's our choice, because the realm of Spirit is founded upon allowance, the freedom to think as we please. Because of allowance, no benevolent being would (or even could) take the freedom of choice away from us. Not even God. The law of allowance can't make a lie true; it just says we're allowed to believe in one if we want to.

On our path to True Healing and spiritual liberation, we need to learn to do as Spirit does. We need to allow. Even though our illness is an expression of something that is not our highest truth, it won't work to request the presence of Spirit in our lives to heal us, yet fight, punish, judge, blame, or contort our experiences. When something arises, desirable or undesirable, we can allow it to show itself without judgment or manipulation. By fully allowing our circumstances, we're not running from our karma.

This is neutrality, and is one of the highest vibrations we can have in this human form. Neutrality isn't a lack of sensation or feeling. Rather, it's a quality that can be *applied* to any sensation or feeling. Getting neutral doesn't mean we have to suck it up or pretend we actually like our painful experiences. It just means that we acknowledge them, whether we like them, love them, or hate them.

What we experience in human form is sometimes so painful it seems there could be absolutely nothing "neutral" about it. What's so neutral about pain? What's so neutral about depression? Ironically, the more we experience pain or apathy (or lameness, tiredness, anxiety, boredom, loneliness, you fill in the blank) without judgment, the more we see Spirit's original signal of love under it.

The opposite of allowance is fighting, fixing, and addiction to improvement. These are fear-based expectations forced onto the body, often in the guise of spiritual healing. In these efforts, we actually end up bypassing the corrections Spirit has for us. There's a difference between True Healing and fixing. Wholeness is a lot more than just the absence of physical disease or symptoms. In this spiritual practice, we don't try to eradicate the ego or our symptoms. Instead, we simply notice the ego's presence and its effects upon us.

Witnessing with allowance—looking truthfully at our situation—allows Spirit to enter and heal. If we can't recognize the problem, we can't allow the solution. Spirit only shows up where there's willingness to see the truth. In order to see Spirit with us, we need to look at our entire situation with openness and curiosity. This is allowance. Without it, we're caught in a vicious cycle that goes nowhere, or more accurately, that goes to the same place over and over again.

THE GUEST HOUSE

This being human is a guest house.
Every morning a new arrival.

A joy, a depression, a meanness,
some momentary awareness comes
as an unexpected visitor.

Welcome and entertain them all!
Even if they are a crowd of sorrows
who violently sweep your house
empty of its furniture,
still, treat each guest honorably.
He may be clearing you out
for some new delight.

The dark thought, the shame, the malice,
meet them at the door laughing
and invite them in.

Be grateful for whatever comes,
because each has been sent
as a guide from beyond.

~Rumi

Learning to allow and let your karma be doesn't mean giving up all action or becoming a pacifist in the healing process. Like a walk along your Red Carpet, it takes volition, vigilance, courage, and compassion. True Healing is not a "lose ten pounds in ten days" kind of diet. A tremendous amount of energy goes toward upholding the ego and our current perceptions about who we are and the illness we're holding. Since there's so much that keeps us in this game, we need vigilance to get us out.

Buddha's physical incarnations were not lacking in trial, error, and practice. He made many futile attempts before he developed a practice that brought him to his enlightenment. Jesus, too. Every spiritualist who has lived and breathed in the world of the ego underwent the rigmarole of coming out of it. But they learned how to let go of the struggle. They learned how to allow.

Teachers like Jesus and Buddha were highly active, powerful, and influential people. Yet they taught peace, love, forgiveness, and tolerance. These qualities are allowing by nature. But these teachers were not passive, by any stretch of the imagination. They were diligent in their practices and ideals, and their efforts were reflected in their spiritual accomplishments and their ability to share with others what they attained for themselves. With any practice, there's some doing involved. Yet the doing itself is passive.

For example, Part III of this book contains a five-step practice that helps initiate the release of stored karma arising from the body. It takes a little conscious effort to learn the steps and then to actually do it each day, but once inside the space of the practice, you can let be. Doing too much or trying too hard is always counterproductive.

That's because stored karma only moves when it's ready to budge. Yet, if the karma isn't ready to go and we don't get results, we feel defeated. Trying to remove karmically incomplete pain or emotion is like trying to trick a dog into the bathtub. He's too smart for that. Karma will stick around until it no longer has a purpose, no matter how hard we try to make it go away.

If an illness is still serving us—if we are still learning from it—it will stay. But as soon as it's ready to move, it will pass from the body. This is why we need to learn allowance. Sometimes we have to let our karma be so that it can release.

Ironically, the more we simply acknowledge karma arising in our bodies without trying to do too much about it, the less charge it has for us. The less charge it has, the easier it is to complete the cycles and move on. In these cases, the "moving on" is usually peaceful, accompanied by a sense of neutrality. "What was the big deal, anyway?" we might ask.

Bringing allowance, neutrality, and forgiveness to the things we hate—like illness or pain—can be a big challenge. It seems counterintuitive. But it's really just counter-*instinctive*. The survival response is rooted heavily in the need to fight or resist.

Please know that I am not suggesting that you move toward harm. But, with a little allowance, you can learn to *lean into* the rattling, unsettling, or disturbing situations that arise so you can take a closer look. Through your allowance, you send an invitation to Spirit and meet the healing process halfway. With practice, your allowance offers the space for Spirit to heal you in the truest sense of the word.

CHAPTER 8

HOW SPIRIT HEALS

Nasrudin was stuck in a terrible flood. Clinging for his life high up in a treetop, he prayed to God for help, "Please, God, come save me from this terrible flood!"

Several hours later, a man floated by on a raft. "Nasrudin!" he yelled, "Climb down and we'll float to safety!"

Nasrudin shouted back, "No, thank you. God will come save me from this terrible flood!" So the man on the raft drifted along downstream.

Nasrudin tried even harder this time and spent his long hours praying in earnest: "Dear God, please come save me from this terrible flood!"

Several hours later, a small motorboat packed with survivors approached Nasrudin's tree. One of the passengers saw Nasrudin and shouted, "Nasrudin! Climb down and we'll float to safety!"

Having devout faith in the hands of God, Nasrudin held tight to his branch and yelled, "No, thank you. God will come save me from this terrible flood!" And so the boat and its occupants floated along downstream.

"What am I doing wrong?" Nasrudin asked. "I must pray even harder so that God will hear me this time." So Nasrudin repeated his mantra one thousand times: "God will come save me from this terrible flood. God will come save me from this terrible flood."

Several more hours passed and he heard the whoosh and chop of a rescue helicopter hovering over him. As the ladder dropped between the branches, the rescue team yelled down, "Nasrudin! Climb up and we'll fly to safety!"

By this time, Nasrudin was tired, dehydrated, and hungry. Yet his devotion was unwavering. He muffled a raspy call through the canopy: "No, thank you. God will come save me from this terrible flood!" And so the helicopter flew off.

That night, Nasrudin died of exhaustion. Upon entering the Pearly Gates, he came face to face with God. Forsaken, Nasrudin pleaded to know why God didn't come and save him from that terrible flood.

God looked Nasrudin squarely in the eye and said, "What are you talking about, Nasrudin? I sent you a raft, a boat, and a helicopter."

As a medical intuitive and Christ healer, I work with people who suffer with chronic, debilitating illness. One of the most heartbreaking things I hear from my clients is that they feel like Spirit has abandoned them. I felt that way too when I was sick. I prayed so hard and tried so hard, but Spirit just didn't return my call. Why wasn't Spirit there when I needed it the most?

Expectation, that's why.

I can confidently say that we should all expect Spirit to show up for us. *That* kind of expectation is a given. But the problem starts when we expect Spirit to show up in a certain way. In poor Nasrudin's case, he expected the Hand of God itself to part the clouds and lift him up to safety.

If we hold onto our preconceived ideas of how Spirit should communicate with us and how it will heal us, we'll likely overlook Spirit's presence, even though it's right in front of us like a giant purple elephant with pink polka dots holding a flashing neon sign. Spirit never chooses to dismiss or overlook us, but with expectation, it's likely going to feel that way.

When I was a child, Jesus—my spiritual teacher and guide—communicated with me through objects: prayer books, flowers, flickering lights, advent calendars, moths and insects, even tables and chairs and other inanimate objects. He was a good friend and good communicator, and I knew him exceptionally well.

At some point as I got older, the communication ended. Or so it seemed. By the time I was into my teens, I thought he must have left me behind, that I was no longer good enough for him, or that I had been imagining it all. I made every effort to try to get him to talk to me again. I used meditation, prayer, channeling, hallucinogenic drugs, even shouting and cursing his name. Nothing worked.

It wasn't until I was well into my twenties that I realized that I was the one who decided to block communication from him, not the other way around. I was harboring a desperate and pathological need to have him tell me exactly what I wanted to hear and nothing else. My adult mind wanted logical evidence of his existence in his enlightened, ethereal form. I wanted historical data about his lifetime as Jesus. I wanted him to show up for me in corporeal form. To him, this must have been like inviting him to high tea while holding my hands over my ears and screaming, "Blah blah blah blah!"

Looking back at the conversations I had with Jesus as a child, I never placed expectations on him, made him out to be what he wasn't, or put my own words in his mouth. Instead, we had a natural exchange of communication—nothing overly special, nothing too noteworthy, just communication for communication's sake. It was an expression of Spirit in the physical realm.

Once I dropped my expectations, my dialogue with him began again. I now work with Jesus very closely on personal and spiritual levels, as well as in my healing sessions with clients. Only now I allow him to share what he wants to share, whether or not it makes sense to my rational mind. Our conversations are once again friendly, open, warm, and trustful.

A decision to heal with Spirit doesn't mean it will happen on the ego's terms or meet our expectations. In fact, if we don't set the ego's terms aside, we'll set Spirit's aside instead. We don't just decide mentally that we want to heal and then something "special" happens. Usually, the clouds don't part as God comes down to save us. Instead, we gradually, steadily, increasingly start to recognize Spirit as it shows up for us in each and every moment.

I am not here to dictate how Spirit will show up for you. You have your own spiritual vibration, spiritual intention, and spiritual direction. You also have your own guides and friends in the Spirit Realm. But I can help you create the space to observe and explore your connection with Spirit while you walk along your Red Carpet. From the space of allowance, Spirit is permitted to show up and heal you. How it shows up? How it heals? Let's let Spirit decide.

SPIRITUAL EXPECTATIONS: 10 WAYS WE CHOOSE AGAINST SPIRIT

1. We want lofty informational pieces all at once.

2. We want overnight miracles, instant gratification, and validation.

3. We want Spirit to fix the body, without asking it to heal the soul.

4. We want Spirit to show up like it does for (insert famous mystic, spiritual teacher, or guru here).

5. We want to get something out of it that elevates us or make us feel special.

6. We want Spirit to have a certain hue, a certain obvious feeling, or a certain predetermined quality.

7. We want Spirit to prove itself to us by showing us something tangible, something we can see with the naked eye.

8. We want Spirit to make something "happen" for us or for someone else.

9. We want the same results we got when a miracle showed up for us the last time.

10. We want Spirit to be something other than what it actually is.

I often say that nothing does the healing but Spirit. Nothing else can heal because nothing but Spirit remains whole. At the same time, True

Healing is not necessarily "faith healing" in the sense that I think we all should abandon our physicians and healers or abort our exercise routines, prescriptions, diet plans, or any physical, mental, emotional, psychological, or energetic approaches we use. Spirit heals in as many ways as there are beings in this entire universe and beyond.

Since Spirit is the foundation of all we are, Spirit permeates all we are. The key to healing is your ability to walk along the Red Carpet, the ability to allow. Spirit heals by entering into any space you allow it to enter. "Space" in this context means anything you give intention to. Intentional space could be something palpable like the physical space of your body or the food or dietary supplements you take. It could also be the thought-space between you and a doctor you work with. It could be the mental or emotional space you set for meditation or prayer. If Spirit is given permission to enter *any* space, it can use that space as a viable means for healing. Since Spirit shows up everywhere, there's no need to drop the healing methods you value or enjoy, or to end the search for a medical approach that could eventually bring positive results on the physical level.

Tracy, a client of mine, recently told me she gave up her seemingly endless, futile search for outside help in regard to healing her vertigo. "No one knows what's wrong with me. I guess it's an inside job." I agreed: True Healing requires inner work.

But I also asked her to keep her eye open to all possibilities—inside, outside, and even to ideas she thought she had already exhausted. Seeing that her soul was already in the process of True Healing, I wanted to remind her that Spirit shows up in unexpected ways.

At our next session, I mentioned that I suspected a deep infection in Tracy's body. She told me that she recently saw an intuitive health practitioner who also informed her that she might have an infection in her jaw. After hearing "infection" a second time, she thought she'd better get it checked out.

Sure enough, an oral surgeon validated the intuitive findings. Tracy had cavitations in several areas of her jaw, likely the result of a long-term infection.

After her initial treatment, Tracy's symptoms decreased significantly, and she reported that her body felt much better and lighter. "I gave up hope that anyone or anything could help me," she said. "There was an opening, and I'm amazed how Spirit showed up for me in such a surprising way."

I had a similar experience in healing my Lyme Disease. After I received the diagnosis, I didn't attempt to treat it right away. Intuitively, none of the most common treatment methods struck me as the right choice. I didn't want antibiotics, not because I tend to veer away from them as a medical approach, but because I just "knew" they wouldn't work. Under such dire circumstances and with such an insidious infection, I honestly would have taken antibiotics if I believed they'd have done the trick for me. But I knew that route wasn't my answer.

There were alternative choices too; some of these I followed, but not to eradicate the infection. Instead, I used them as detoxification methods to clear my liver, my gut, and all my cells so that when the infection was ready to leave, my body would be able to handle the upsurge of immune activity and bacterial die-off.

One day, while I was a student in a nutrition training, I met a teacher who had successfully recovered from Lyme Disease (twice) using a series of very strong botanical formulas designed specifically for the Lyme bacteria and its coinfections.[1] As soon as I heard the name of the formulas, my heart opened and I thought, "This is it."

I researched the formulas, figured out how to get them, and planned out a four-month eradication program.

I was as sick as a dog in those four months. I was on the verge of throwing up and fainting all the time, pain permeated my body, and I was in a constant state of depression. At the same time, a spark inside me knew it was working. Spirit was so close to me in that time. Deep inside my soul, a light broke through the cracks. I could see myself healing.

The botanical formulas I used are not magic potions. Like all treatments, they don't work for everyone. I give a lot of credit to these formulas, but the magic element was that I was ready; my soul had begun the process of True Healing. I cleared some karma and my body responded. Just the right solution came at just the right time.

True Healing often happens like this, step by step. Although True Healing, wholeness, and enlightenment are accessible to us in an instant, it just doesn't happen until the soul is totally primed and ready. For most of us, it takes the

---

[1] Byron White Formulas: ByronWhiteFormulas.com

soul a while—like many lifetimes and between-life experiences—to adjust to the idea of letting go of its identity with the ego. The soul is still afraid of losing what it thinks it has in the ego.

True Healing usually happens by removing one brick in a wall at a time; we're not ready to have the wrecking ball come in and take the whole foundation down all at once. Instead, we carefully and intentionally chisel away the mortar that holds each brick in place. One brick at a time, we gradually see the light that gleams in from the other side. The light blinds and frightens us at first, but we eventually realize what we've been missing without it. It's the chicken soup and warm blanket on a cold, gloomy day.

PART III

TRUE HEALING IN ACTION

CHAPTER 9

THE TRUE HEALING MEDITATION

What comes to mind when I say the word "meditation"? Sitting cross-legged on a cushion? Holding your hands in prayer? Chanting? Visualization? Thinking positive thoughts? Sitting frozen like a statue of the Buddha for a really long time? There are many forms of meditation, but it's unlikely that the one I will outline in this section came to your mind.

The True Healing Meditation is specifically designed for people who struggle with illness, pain, injury, trauma, symptoms, and the intense emotions that arise from being diagnosed with disease. With this practice, you don't have to worry about struggling with things like staying still, keeping your spine straight, or thinking good thoughts. I didn't like that kind of mental and physical gymnastics in my meditation practice when I was sick, and I'm assuming you don't either.

Meditating got harder and harder for me when I was sick, mainly because I was in such pain. Sitting upright and holding myself there made my joints hurt and created more frustration rather than relaxation for me. I found I was much more comfortable lying down rather than upright and unsupported. Eventually I adopted the lying-down position as my go-to meditation posture. For your comfort while healing, the True Healing Meditation is performed lying down or in any position that is most suitable for you.

The True Healing Meditation is a real-life practice. It does not attempt to transcend your situation—the fact that you struggle right now, that you are in physical or emotional pain, and that you suffer with illness. It is not a visualization practice in the sense that you try to see yourself in a better place, with a better body, or living a better life. It simply brings you into the present moment with how (and who) you are right now. You get to touch in with your body, your mind, your soul, and Spirit exactly as they would show themselves in the here and now.

This includes paying witness to the gross and subtle pain in your body, as well as the fear signals of your ego. But with daily practice, you'll also get to know first-hand the spacious, healing energies of Spirit as they work their way through your soul, and all the way into the container of your physical form.

GETTING STARTED

The True Healing Meditation is divided into five steps. Each step helps you bring your conscious awareness into your body and gets you onto the Red Carpet of allowance so that you can readily call upon Spirit for True Healing. From there, the body responds.

The five steps are:

1. Anchor the body to the Earth
2. Scan the four quadrants of the body for pain, symptoms, or intense emotion
3. Go into the hotspot and deepen your body-scan
4. Find the call for love
5. Invite Spirit to heal

The next chapters provide detailed explanations of each step. Once you have read through the flow and structure of the full True Healing Meditation, you may use the abbreviated version in Appendix A.

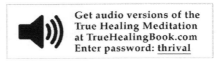

Get audio versions of the True Healing Meditation at TrueHealingBook.com Enter password: thrival

Ideally, the True Healing Meditation is done every day. It's a way for you to spend time with yourself just as you are—to love yourself, respect yourself, forgive yourself, and heal yourself. It's your spiritual self-care. The full practice takes about thirty minutes and may be done any time of the day.

You may think a daily practice is challenging; there's no time, no space, and no support. That may be true if you are looking for these outside of yourself. There might not be anyone else that will give you the time, space, or support. *You* have to create those. And that can be hard at first if you come from a family or social network that doesn't value spiritual work or meditation. In this case, you're the group leader, the pioneer that forges ahead. You need conviction and strong intention to do the practice. You need to set the space and time for it, both physically and mentally.

Setting the space

Use a quiet room where you can shut the door for privacy. If you are able to dedicate an entire room just for meditation, fantastic! Most of us aren't so lucky. My meditation room functions as a classroom where I hold my online telecourses and healing sessions. It's also the guest bedroom and my office.

All you need is a little space on the floor or a bed to lie down with knees up. You may have to move some furniture around to accommodate. I do my meditation on the floor at the foot of the bed. I keep a light blanket draped over the footboard, and a throw pillow nearby that I tuck under my head if needed.

I personally don't care too much for ritual, so I don't have a shrine or altar. But my meditation room has a peaceful, meditative tone to it. Earthy colors ground me and make me feel safe, so my practice space has lots of earth tones and wood furniture. You may prefer a watery or ethereal feel, or a Zen-like minimalistic atmosphere. In any case, choose colors and accessories that make you feel safe, supported, or spiritually uplifted. Try to set it up so that just walking into the room feels like a healing to you.

Setting the time

The True Healing Meditation requires about thirty minutes for your formal daily practice. I recommend picking a time to do your practice each day and sticking with that as best you can. What time are you least likely to be disturbed by children, phone calls, or business matters? That's a good time to meditate.

I also suggest you put your practice sessions into your calendar, just as you would a date, a yoga class, or a doctor's visit. It's an important part of your day. Although, if you do miss a practice period here and there, don't sweat it. Occasionally missing practice is inevitable.

You can also take intentional integration periods. These are days that you give yourself permission not to practice at all. When I was sick, I liked to take the weekends off. It gave me space to integrate, and took the pressure off the expectation that I had to meditate every day to be a "good" practitioner. Skip the expectation and perfection stuff. You don't need the added stress right now.

I know it's hard to show up to meditate when you're sick. But the more you practice the True Healing Meditation, the more you'll crave the time and space with yourself. You'll *want* to come into your practice space, get into your body, and experience yourself just as you are. Even if your intention is simply to lie down and take a conscious rest period, you'll get tremendous benefit while you're in the process of True Healing.

CHAPTER 10

STEP ONE: ANCHOR THE BODY

In the throes of my illness, I had to pay a visit to the community lab every three or four months for blood work, mostly to monitor my adrenals and erratic thyroid gland. Getting blood drawn is usually the least of all worries for people who struggle with illness. For me, it left me brimming with anxiety.

My fear wasn't so much about the test results. It was due to the high probability that I'd end up passed out on the cold, hard, sterile floor. One minute I would get a needle in my arm, and the next I would wake up with a nurse waving orange juice under my nose like a boxing coach with smelling salts.

Suffice it to say, I don't like needles. Yet skipping the blood work was not an option for me at that delicate time during my illness. My challenge was to find a way to walk in and out of the clinic while remaining relatively non-reactive to the thoughts of the needle before, during, and after the procedure.

My solution was to anchor my body. Instead of trying to bypass my body during the experience, I would go within and do a quick anchoring meditation. I would also ask the nurse to set me up in a recliner so I could lay back and close my eyes, and would request that she didn't try to distract me with a flurry of questions.

It worked. I haven't passed out from a blood draw ever since.

An anchor line or grounding cord is an energetic connection between the body and the Earth below. Anchoring acts as a ground wire for excitable energy or emotion in your body. Just as a wall socket or a lightning rod needs a ground, the physical body needs a place to discharge energy so it doesn't blow a circuit. Anchoring to the earth gives the body an avenue to clear itself of built up, pent up, super-charged energy.

Anchoring also relaxes the survival instinct. When the body is ungrounded, the mind-body tends to react to stimulus and go into fear. This is what would happen when I would faint. I would anticipate the needle and unconsciously envision myself passing out. Just walking into the clinic, the sights and smells of the place, provoked my anxiety. My fight or flight response was turned on even before sitting down for the draw. When the fight or flight response is turned on, anchoring is the number one "go to" tool. It helps the body to immediately wind down and relieve itself of survival-based thoughts.

Anchoring also keeps awareness in the body. It keeps you present in the here and now, even during times of stress or fear. It helps you learn to stay instead of leaving the body out of fear. Like an anchor that keeps a boat from floating off to sea, an anchor for the body keeps your awareness from floating away from your body.

ANCHORING THE BODY

Start the practice lying down on the floor, a mat, a couch, or a bed. Keep your eyes closed and your attention turned inward on your body.

Have your knees up and propped against each other. (If your condition doesn't allow you to relax on your back comfortably, any relaxed posture is welcome.) Spend a moment making micro-adjustments, creating a sturdy tripod between the feet, knees, and hips. This position induces relaxation and supports the hips and lower back.

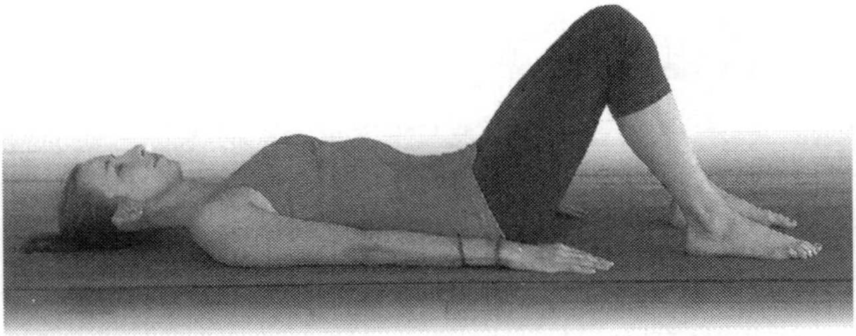

Figure 1: True Healing Meditation Posture[2]

There are seven anchor points for this exercise: the two sit bones, the two shoulder blades, the back of the head, and the two feet.

Hip anchors

Start by finding your sit bones. These are the two rounded bony structures at the back and bottom of the hips that take the weight of your body when sitting. The sit bones are the part of the lower hips that look like raccoon eyes or Zorro's mask in anatomy books; they each have a large, round gap that accommodates the nerves that run from the hips down into the legs. To find the

[2] Photo courtesy pilatesbodyworkout.com

sit bones in a lying-down posture, feel into the large pressure point at the back of the hips that takes the weight of your body. This is your sacral bone. Move your awareness down and to the sides of this central pressure point. These are your sit bones.

Then make an energetic anchor from your sit bones all the way down to the center of the planet, through all the sub-layers and deep into the core of the earth. Use your psychic imagination to make this connection. Use any imagery that works for you: an anchor, a beam of light, a magnetic pull, a tree trunk, a waterfall. If visualization distracts you, simply intend that your body roots itself to the Earth below.

Shoulder blade anchors

Then move your awareness up to the shoulder blades on either side of the upper spine. Just as you did with the sit bones, imagine an anchor line from the shoulder blades all the way down to the center of the planet.

As you ground the anchor points, you may feel a subtle sense of connection, of "touch-down," or a weighty, gravitational tug on your body. You might feel as light as a feather. Or you may feel nothing at all. Just stay present with your body, noticing any obvious, subtle, or neutral sensations in your body as you anchor.

Head anchor
Move your awareness to the spot where the back of your head meets the floor. Feel the weight of your head against the floor. Then, using an image or an intention, create an anchor line from your head to the center of the planet.

Feet anchors
Lastly, add the feet. Bring your awareness to both feet at the same time and imagine them rooted, connected and anchored into the Earth deep below.

All anchors
Take a conscious breath and feel all the anchor points at the same time: Your sit bones, your shoulder blades, your head, and your feet. How would you describe your response? Is there an emotional element, like calmness, peacefulness or clarity? Does your body resist or fight the experience? Try not to judge your body's responses; just observe them.

Finally, discharge built up karma around any of the anchor points (karma might be experienced as pain, tension, discomfort, or intense emotions) by imagining small pebbles or river rocks. Imagine putting the karmic energy into the pebbles and drop the pebbles down your anchor lines.

Complete the practice by sitting up gently for a few moments before opening your eyes and going about your day. If you plan to continue to step two of the five-step practice, stay in the lying-down position and move on.

CHAPTER 11

STEP TWO: SCAN THE QUADRANTS

After setting the intention to come into your body and relax the survival responses through anchoring, the next step is to briefly run your awareness through your whole body to detect the places where you hold karma—the areas that express chronic or intense pain, aggravating symptoms, or intense emotions.

Some of these holding places may be quite obvious, but as you gain experience at scanning, you'll also come across subtle sensations, feelings, and vibrations. This is karma behind the scenes; the underlying stuff that's barely at the surface of consciousness. Sensing both the gross and subtle sensations in the body is of utmost importance in this work. Your awareness of your stored karma allows it to ultimately release from the body.

Scanning begins with dividing your body into four quadrants, sweeping your awareness through each one, looking for marked areas that hold tension or symptoms, as well as areas that are relaxed, pain-free, or neutral. At the end of your initial body scan, you'll hone in on one hotspot for the healing work. A "hotspot" is a targeted area in the body that holds energy, karma, pain, tension, stress, or intense emotion.

Since uprisings of pain or emotion come and go, hotspots may change day-to-day and moment-to-moment. Yet, most of us have a proclivity to recurring karmic themes. The same sensations often pop up again and again, in the same quadrants and with the same emotional fabric. Body scanning practice helps you see your recurrent karmic patterns.

SCANNING THE QUADRANTS

As you move through each quadrant, imagine heightening the feeling-sensors in your body, bringing the skin, the muscles, organs, and tissues to life so you can become more acutely aware of any and all sensations in the scanning areas. You may even want to imagine each area breathing itself, as if each cell in the body has its own set of lungs.

Start and end in any quadrant you wish, just make sure to sweep through each with equal attention.

Quadrant 1: Feet, calves, and thighs

Sweep your awareness through the bottoms of the feet, tops of the feet, toes, and ankles, noticing sensations of any kind (tingling, aching, swelling) in this relatively small, localized area. Just spend a moment or so here, then move up to your calves and shins. Notice the difference between the fleshiness of your calf muscles and the sharpness of the shinbone at the front.

And then move up to your thighs, front and back. These are very large, very powerful muscles. If you pay attention, you might find some obvious fatigue or tension here. Notice the difference in sensations between the right and the left thigh, and between the thighs, the calves, and the feet.

Now get a sense of both legs, top and bottom, all at once. What one area expresses the most sensation?

Quadrant 2: Pelvis, hips, and belly

Next, move your awareness up to the hips and pelvis. Start by feeling into the bony parameters of the hip and pelvic bones; these make a bowl or container for the organs in the lower belly. See if you can sense this container. Then scan the soft tissue inside the bowl all around the bony rim, looking for any physical pain, fatigue, or tension inside the bowl. Also notice the areas in the pelvic bowl that are pain-free, symptom-free, or neutral.

Feel around the backside into the muscle attachments of the buttocks and hips. Feel for deep or superficial strain or pain here on either side. Fatigue is common in these areas.

Then move up to the upper belly, and scan for any gross or subtle painful physical sensations all around the gut, the small intestines, and colon. Because the gut has its own nervous system, it often houses significant expressions of karma. Look for mild or intense pain, bloating, pulling, or cramping. Make sure to also sense the neutral zones, the areas that do not hold tension or pain right now.

Then move around to the lower back, sensing the difference between the pliability of the belly and the rigid structure of the lower spine. Are the muscles on either side of the lower back gripping or holding?

Now expand your scan to sense the entire pelvic, hip, and belly region, all at once, front and back. Is there a particular area in this quadrant that holds more sensation for you than the others?

Quadrant 3: Chest, shoulders, and arms

Now move your awareness into the area under the ribcage. The ribcage protects the upper digestive organs (stomach, pancreas, liver) as well as the heart and lungs. Scan all around under the ribs, from bottom to top, and even in between each of the ribs. Does the ribcage expand and contract easily and loosely with the breath? Or does it seem to tighten and restrict the movement?

Scan for pockets of pain and discomfort all around the chest area. Pain can be dull or sharp, aching or piercing, or anything in between. Notice where there's flow, freedom, movement, or openness in the chest area. Then scan up into the collarbones.

Now move around to the backside to feel into the shoulder blades. Then into the trapezius muscles that run along the top of the shoulders. These areas are notorious for holding stress and tension. Sweep down both arms and hands, too.

Are there any old injuries or arthritic pains in the arms and hands?

Now sense quadrants one, two, and three together as a unit to get a sense for the overall fabric of sensation in this larger area. Where are you holding the most significant pain or discomfort?

Quadrant 4: Neck and head

Then move into the neck, scanning the front, the sides, and the back. Pain can show up as heat, pulling, pushing, gripping, holding, aching, straining. Notice if your neck is expressing any of these pain sensations right now.

Then move inward, into the throat, mouth, and jaw. Do you feel any soreness or coarseness in the throat? Notice how your tongue sits inside the mouth. And is the jaw clenching?

Now sweep up into the nose and sinus cavities. Feel the coolness of your breath gliding in and out. Take your awareness into the eyes and forehead. Are your eyes and forehead muscles straining? You might grip and strain around these areas without even being aware of it.

Lastly, sweep your awareness through the brain, the center of head, and around the perimeter of the skull. See if you can feel your brain pressing against your skull. You may notice a mild headache or a high-pitched hum that you didn't notice before. This is natural and normal.

Of all the areas in this smaller region of the neck and head, which area is most noticeably holding pain or tension?

Full-body scan

Now notice all four quadrants at once. Notice the different textures, colors, and qualities, as if you were running your eyes and fingers over a patchwork quilt. Do certain sections have a different look or feel than the others? Are there defined zones of pain, pleasure, and neutrality? Can you tell where one feeling-sensation in the body begins and another ends?

Now pick one area in any of the quadrants that is expressing pain, emotion, or discomfort, or any area in the body you'd like to hone in on for a deeper scan. You'll work with this particular area for the rest of the practice.

Say hello to your anchor lines again at the hips, shoulder blades, head, and feet. Imagine putting some of the arising karma (pain, emotion, or intensity) into small river rocks or pebbles. Drop the pebbles down your anchor lines.

If you plan on continuing to step three, stay in the lying-down position and move on.

CHAPTER 12

STEP THREE: GO INTO THE HOTSPOT

After doing a brief but thorough scan of all four quadrants and determining which karmic hotspot you'd like to work with, you're ready to move on to step three. This step takes you into the subtlety of the felt sense that underlies the pain or emotion your body is presenting. The "felt sense"—a term coined by Eugene Gendlin from his book *Focusing*—is a culmination of energy, feeling, and sensation. It's the innate wisdom of the body-mind, the communication of the soul expressed through the physical form. The felt sense is one of the access points to the soul's karma.

If you felt a little rushed or shallow in your initial body scan, tapping into the felt sense is the opportunity to dive a little deeper into the ocean of your body. Think of the felt sense as the sub-surface current that moves your entire body and mind. Diving beneath the deep surges and swells of pain or intense emotion—and under the superficial cresting and breaking of your reactions *to* them—reveals the tidal motion of the felt sense.

In order to experience the nature of the felt sense of the body, you first must set the intention of allowance. Remember to step onto your Red Carpet as you move into a deeper exploration of karma that's expressing itself through your body. On the Red Carpet, you are totally safe yet remain totally present to what's going on within and without you. Allow your pains, fears, hopes, symptoms, darkness, lightness, desires, dreams, and demons to show up on the sidelines. While walking with allowance along your centerline, you give your body permission to share its story.

The True Healing Meditation consciously shines your light onto the things that want to stay hidden in your body and mind. Staying with the felt sense brings your karma out of the darkness of your storehouse consciousness and into the light of day. Envisioning yourself on the Red Carpet helps you stay centered and neutral under uncomfortable and sometimes frightening conditions. Pain, fear, or any number of emotions or sensations may show up as you venture into your hotspot. Remind yourself to stay neutral by imagining yourself walking along your Red Carpet. There, you have a safe vantage point to observe without judgment. You are abiding the law of allowance.

Once you have established your willingness to observe your body with allowance, you can start to go deeper into the felt sense of your chosen hotspot, honing in on a specific, targeted area that holds pain, sensation, symptoms, or emotion.

Our natural instinct is to ride "on top" of our pain or intensity, without spelunking deeper inside the body to really feel it out. When we do this, we sacrifice our opportunity to experience what the pain is really trying to say in present-time. Instead, we rely on our previous thoughts about the pain, forming a superficial idea about what it is and why it's there. Our previous ideas were likely based in fear: "This pain means I'm sick and unhealthy"; "This pain will last for days or weeks or months"; "This pain is associated with this illness." The more we make snap and superficial assumptions about the pain, the more the pain gets programmed into our subconscious minds. This cascading process can make us perpetually sick.

Pain, symptoms, sensations, and emotions are born to shift and change. Step three gets you into the direct experience of what's happening in your body *right now*. It makes no assumptions about what was before or what will be in the future. It keeps you present—right here, right now—inside the container of the physical body. In this space, you allow your symptom or sensation to move, change, and heal.

GOING INTO THE HOTSPOT

Find the location

From the relaxed lying-down posture, notice the details of your chosen hotspot. Gently move your awareness into the symptom, sensation, or feeling, gathering as much in-depth information as you can about its location in the body. Ask yourself these questions, and feel along as you go:

- Where is this symptom or sensation geographically located in my body? Does it have an epicenter or a bulls-eye? Does it radiate outward from this core in all directions or does the sensation protrude to one side?

- What shape does it have and what size is it? Is it blobby or spiky? Round or non-symmetrical? Does it take over a large area, like my entire abdomen or the entire side of my body? Or is it in a relatively small, confined location?
- What does my hotspot feel like at the perimeter of the sensation? What kind of boundary does this sensation have? Solid or fuzzy? Does it gradually taper off at some point? Does it feel different as it progresses outward and away from the central location?
- Does the sensation extend out into my energy field? Does it seem to go beyond my physical body in some way?

Describe the texture

Go deeper into this sensation or symptom now and see if you can get an overall felt sense of its quality. In other words, what does it feel like in the body? Are there words or phrases that could be used to describe the physical texture of this sensation? Here are some ideas:

- Intense | Weak
- Piercing | Dull
- Penetrating | Extending
- Stretching | Contracting
- Hot | Cold
- Throbbing | Continuous
- Pushing | Pulling
- Heavy | Light
- Hard | Soft
- Fixed | Fluid

Notice if the texture of the symptom or sensation fluctuates as you bring your awareness to it. Don't be surprised if it starts to shift, change, or move before your eyes. Often what we think is fixed and firm is actually fluid and pliable. Allow the sensation to disappear and then reappear or move around as you deepen your scan.

Define the emotion

It sometimes feels as if sensation and emotion are two separate entities, but in fact both come from the same source. There is always an emotional characteristic to any physical sensation. Connecting an emotional quality to the sensation helps you build a bridge between these often dissociate elements.

Go deep into the sub-layers of the body now, into the felt sense of the experience. Ask your body what the subtle emotional temperament of the symptom or sensation is. How does it make you *feel* to have this symptom? What is your emotional response to the symptom?

Without thinking too much about the emotion or trying to mentally analyze it, stay with the direct *bodily* experience of the emotion itself. Where do you feel the emotion in the body? Does the emotion have a texture to it, just like the physical sensation does? Can you describe the feeling?

Here are some characteristics you might use to define the emotional quality of your experience:

- Angry | Enraged
- Depressed | Apathetic
- Weary | Apprehensive
- Irritated | Fickle
- Lonely | Abandoned
- Hopeless | Helpless
- Humiliated | Embarrassed
- Guilty | Regretful
- Fearful | Frightened
- Resistant | Rebellious

The more detailed you can get with defining the emotion, the better. An image, a gesture, or a color also works to replace a word if you are having a hard time naming the emotion.

Complete your scan

Finally, ask your body to give you any other details or information about this symptom or sensation. All you have to do is hang out with your sensation, allowing any of the karma you are ready to look at to come forth into your conscious-awareness. You do not need to mentally figure anything out or make anything go away; just see how close you can get to the sensation and its concurring emotion with as much allowance and neutrality as you can.

To finish, take notice of any neighboring areas that are not expressing this particular sensation or emotion. With equanimity, notice the differences in these areas and try not to make a judgment of good or bad. Just witness.

Then bring your awareness again to the anchor points at your two sit bones, two shoulder blades, head, and feet. Take a breath and imagine putting some of the karma that is ready to be released into a few river rocks or pebbles. Drop the pebbles down your anchor lines to help release any karmic buildup.

Complete the practice by sitting up gently for a few moments before opening your eyes and going about your day. If you plan on continuing to step four, stay in the lying-down position and move on.

CHAPTER 13

STEP FOUR: FIND THE CALL FOR LOVE

Needs are reflections of our deepest suffering, of our separation from Spirit. Rather than asking what we instinctively want for the external shell of the body (to be cured of the disease, to be pain-free, or to be rid of this heavy emotion or nagging symptom) ask the *soul* what it needs to heal its perceived lack of wholeness. The soul never requires the body to be well for it to be free of suffering. If suffering starts in the soul, it's the soul that requires the healing, not the body.

Asking the soul what it needs often seems like too big a question: "How could I possibly know what my soul needs? If I knew *that*, I wouldn't be here!" Rather than attempting to come up with the one and only answer that your soul needs for ultimate healing, just find the simple next step to help get you there. Remember, True Healing progresses one baby step at a time, and your soul is walking along a path laid with steppingstones. Each time you find your soul's call for love—its perceived need—in the present moment, you take a step onto a new stone and another step toward True Healing. There's no pressure, expectation, or problem solving in this practice. You don't need to have all the answers right now.

Step four is a time to stay deep inside your body to listen to the wisdom of the felt sense. The purpose of step four is to get the underlying body-feel for the question, "What is my call for love?"

Asking (and answering) this question is not an analytical process. You tap into the bodily knowingness that lies just beneath the thinking mind. Staying with the physical and energetic sensations of the body will help you get your answer in the most intelligent, intuitive way.

FINDING THE CALL FOR LOVE

State the question

"What is the call for love?" can be stated in myriad ways, via words, an image, an intention or a gesture, anything that cues the body to respond intuitively to your query. Use the following phrases to frame your question, or come up with your own:

- What is the 'call for love' that underlies these sensations and emotions?
- What does my soul need in this moment for True Healing?
- What is my perceived lack?
- What would make me feel whole and complete right now?
- What will help me take my next step?

You might also like to come up with an image that sums up the question without using words or phrasing. Send the image out from the mind of your body to the mind of your soul. Any image works. Here are some ideas:

- A receptive hand
- An open vessel

- A question mark
- A rose or a lotus
- A heart
- A pair of wings
- An empty page of a book

Receive the answer

After stating your question or sending your image, stay present inside your body with your body's wisdom. Rest inside your body with its sensations, and gently, intuitively, look for your answer.

You may get your answer in the form of a phrase like, "I need truth" or "I need encouragement." Look for an answer that is rich, deep, poignant, and fresh. What will help your soul take a next step in healing?

If you get an abstract answer, such as "I need love" or "I need healing," see if you can unpack it a little: "Yes, I need love, but what *form* of love do I need right now?" Expressions such as authenticity, nurturing, connection, essence, boldness, or softening might be more descriptive statements for the now of your current situation. Don't be surprised if you come up with a word or a phrase that surprises you, or one that is pithier than what your mental-mind might have provided.

You might also get your answer through an image or a symbol. You might see yourself digging in the dirt, running along the beach, freefalling, holding something, or something holding you. You might see an image of a star, a color, a pathway, a desert sky, a triangle, or a leaf.

Allow any image to show itself, and see if you can get a feeling for what the image or symbol means for you. If you are in the direct experience of your body, there may be a gestalt-like sense that accompanies the word, phrase, or image; you'll understand what the word or image means to you. You might just know the answer intuitively, as if it came to you off the top of your head.

If you do not receive an answer within several minutes or if you find yourself struggling, resisting, or going into effort, take a step back and return to anchoring and scanning the body.

Whether or not you receive an answer right now, you can move on to step five. Briefly become aware of your anchor lines once more, and drop some pebbles down to release any arising karma, and move forward.

CHAPTER 14

STEP FIVE: INVITE SPIRIT TO HEAL

Receiving an answer to your question, "What is my call for love" is a healing in and of itself. Communication from the soul to the body *is* healing. Your answer may have been accompanied by an opening in the body or a sense of understanding. Tears of compassion, goose bumps, and subtle "A-ha" moments may be common for you in this practice. But alas, as soon as the question is answered, a new one arises: "What am I supposed to *do* with it?"

It's typical for the ego-mind to think that since it has received some valuable information, it must now figure out exactly what to do to achieve what is "supposed" to come from it. For example, if your call for love was the need for respect, the ego wants to hash out exactly how it's going to get it. "How can I get more respect around here?" it asks.

Unfortunately, this approach isn't going to work, because the respect you need—or the tenderness, new vision, honesty, purity, or whatever it is your soul needs right now—doesn't come from outside sources. It comes from the inside first, from Spirit. Only when you are able to receive what you need from the Original Source will you begin to experience what you need all around you in your outer world. Receiving what you need from Spirit is like a seed planted deep within the soul that sprouts through the fertile soil up into the world. True Healing begins when you allow Spirit to meet your needs for you, and then let it grow up and out.

Here, you're allowing Spirit to carry out its solution—the function of True Healing—through your mind and all the way out into your physical existence. Step five is a space to set an intention for True Healing, as well as to witness first hand a felt sense of your own essence as Spirit in the physical body.

One way to get a feeling-sense of Spirit in the body is through the frequencies of color and light. Every color in the spectrum has a spiritual vibration underneath it. Spirit often uses rays of light to help us take our next steps in healing.

All colors come with an almost palpable aura to them that affect us in some way. Colors provoke emotional and energetic responses; they have psychophysical affects upon the body and mind.

Think of the color pink, for example. Notice the subtle response you have toward it. Can you almost feel the color in some subtle way? Does the color engage you somehow?

Now switch to gold and notice the difference in how your body responds to this frequency. Do you respond differently than you did to the pink frequency? Can you describe the difference?

Now see a ray of purple. What affect does this color frequency have on you emotionally, mentally, or energetically? Can you sense the difference between purple, gold, and pink?

Now sense teal. Now sky blue. Now white. If you could describe how each of these colors affects you, what would you say in a word or two?

For clairaudient people—musicians, sound healers, and those who receive spiritual communication through words or verbal telepathy—Spirit might heal through tones, sound vibrations, rhythms, or spoken word.

In many spiritual traditions, it is said that the current of sound is the basis for all life; it is the stream of energy that flows from the heart of the Universal Mind to the heart of the all. Consider yourself blessed if you are one of the few who are able to tap into a direct sound healing from Spirit.

Spirit also heals through feelings or a sense of being energetically touched. A healing presence may sweep through you, embrace you, or nudge you in some subtle or profound way. You might even pick up a healing thought or vision.

From an esoteric perspective, our needs and desires have a frequency or a wavelength. One of the ways Spirit heals is by matching a wavelength of light, sound, or feeling with the wavelength of need. It offers the underlying *spiritual vibration* to help fulfill the soul's perceived lack. It uses these vibrations to fill in where you think you are not whole. These vibrations penetrate through the all the levels of the mind—through the soul and all the way into the cells of the physical body.

Remain open to the healing in the present moment; it may show up in a new and different form every time you engage in your practice. How does Spirit show itself to you when you allow it to come as it would right now, without manipulation or expectation?

RECEIVING YOUR HEALING

Staying inside the container of your body and connecting with the deeper felt sense, ask Spirit to give you a healing that can help you, as a soul in a body, take a next step. Let Spirit give you a balm for your soul's present-time call for love.

Allow Spirit to offer you a color, a sound, a feeling, a thought, or anything that shows you its healing presence. If your need is for security, what provides you with the *spiritual vibration* of security? If your need is for help, what provides you with the *spiritual vibration* of help? Enlightened guessing works here: what color or sound or feeling most naturally seems like a healing for you right now?

Allow that to penetrate your body as you receive it in the soul. It might come in like a wave or a bath, or like warm nectar through your tissues. Notice where in your body the healing penetrates.

Does it go right to your hotspot? Does it go somewhere else first? Does it flood the whole body from the top down or from the bottom up? Or is it already there inside of you, permeating your being from the inside out? Try not to control where it comes from or where it goes; let Spirit do the work. It will bring the healing exactly where it needs to go right now.

What does the healing feel like in your body? Does it initiate a certain response? Does the vibration subtly affect your emotional, mental, or energetic tone?

Spend a few moments soaking up this spiritual vibration in your body. Allow the healing to be as delicate or as distinct as it wants to be. Trust that Spirit is working through you now and that the work is happening at the soul-level, not just in the body.

To finish, briefly scan the hotspot area again, noticing any textural changes there. Do you react a little differently toward the symptoms or sensations? Is there a shift in your body or mind? Do you greet the hotspot with a little more neutrality or compassion?

Say hello to the seven anchor lines again—the two sit bones, the two shoulder blades, the head, and both feet. Drop some pebbles down the anchor lines to let go of any stored karma that is ready to be discharged and released.

Carefully sit up, stretch your arms overhead, and take a deep breath before getting up and going about your day.

CHAPTER 15

TRUE HEALING AS A PRACTICE

Gathering information is a big part of the spiritual path. Reading books, listening to lectures, receiving instruction, and being guided through the practices by an experienced teacher are foundational for your spiritual growth. You have to lay the conceptual groundwork in order to understand why you are practicing it in the first place.

At the same time, knowledge only really increases as you practice what you're taught. *You* have to do it, not watch someone else do it or have someone else do it for you.

Many seekers get caught in the game of going from one spiritual self-help book to the next. They try out a practice or a protocol for a while, somewhat superficially, only to discard it after a few weeks or months as soon as the next big thing hits the shelves.

I get it. A book can't really get to the heart of anything substantial; it can only introduce concepts and offer inspiration for further exploration. Yet many self-help teachers do not offer much in the way of furthering the development of the reader, except for what's inside their next self-help book. The reader's natural inclination is to hop over to the next available thing rather than turn the information into a real-life spiritual path.

I'm no guru. I don't claim to have your answers or something that you don't already have. My purpose as a teacher is to offer workable spiritual tools that empower you to find your own answers. I hope you not only find this book conceptually helpful, but that it inspires you to delve deeper into the nature of your spirituality. The best way I know how to do that is through practice. And unfortunately, you can't go deep into practice just by reading a book. It has to become a part of your life.

Life in general is one big spiritual practice, but there are at least three very basic ways to integrate practice aspects of spiritual work within the framework of your daily life. These are:

1. Formal meditation practice
2. Moment-to-moment practice
3. Group retreat practice

We've already discussed the first component in detail. "Formal" here simply means a dedicated time each day to do your work. There's nothing formal about it: no ritual, dress code, or paraphernalia needed. It's just you showing up with yourself—body, mind, and Spirit—in your daily thirty-minute True Healing Meditation.

Moment-to-moment practice

The more you spend dedicated time with yourself in your formal practice periods, the more you'll notice Spirit in your everyday life. Spirit calls gently to you in each and every moment, not just when you've assumed an "official" meditation posture. All you have to do is notice.

You can think of it as saying hello. Spirit always says hello to you, but communication only happens when both parties are willing to greet each other. Your moment-to-moment practice happens any time you consciously say hello to Spirit throughout your day.

When you first start a moment-to-moment practice, you might only remember to say hello to Spirit once or twice on any given day. You forget or get pulled into the drama of daily life. But more space opens up inside you as you progress, and soon you'll find yourself checking in three, four, five times each day. You're less forgetful, or maybe it's because communicating with Spirit becomes more of a necessity. Eventually, Spirit is so much a part of your life, it seems as if it is with you always, guiding you through all you do.

Start just a couple times a day if you can. Say hello to Spirit while cooking, working, walking, driving, or waiting in line. Bring your awareness into your body, and use your hip anchor lines to ground and settle you. Feel into the sensations inside your body. You don't have to close your eyes; right where you, whatever you're doing is the perfect time to say hello. Even if there's pain or aching or irritable emotions, can you also sense the spaciousness of Spirit?

The workbook section from *A Course in Miracles* is a great way to practice the moment-to-moment aspects of spirituality. Everyday you'll get a teaching in the form of a statement or an intention that you can come back to throughout the day to initiate the True Healing of Spirit.

Group retreat practice

The daily thirty-minute practice probably won't take you into profound multidimensional states of spiritual awareness. Sometimes, yes, but probably not every day. Very deep daily contemplation makes it really hard for us as lay practitioners—versus monks, nuns, or ascetics—to maintain the ins and outs of daily life. Deep meditation can catapult us into subsurface-level growth periods that can push us over the spiritual edge at a time when we also have to think about working, cooking, running errands, and taking care of kids (not to mention taking really good care of ourselves while we're healing).

Yet the soul craves immersion into the divine. It wants deep contemplation. On the path of True Healing, it needs more than thirty minutes of your time. It wants to go deeper. It calls for more space. It needs a dedicated retreat.

Group retreats are the perfect antidote for a soul that craves deep and lasting spiritual growth. Retreats offer the serenity of a peaceful surrounding and a harmonious vibration to sit in for a while. Teachers are there to offer instruction, and fellow students to offer camaraderie. There are even workers to provide food and nourishment.

After practicing anything for some time, we often become complacent with the tools or hit plateaus in our learning. It's hard to move forward without some support and motivation. Getting together with a seasoned teacher and an intentional, like-minded group in a practice-type setting will take you to a new level. You'll get off your plateau and out of your comfort zone, and will forge ahead into new uncharted territory. Your soul can again move and grow.

If you do not feel well enough to participate in a retreat, wait. It can be overly stressful to go into a retreat setting if you are very sick or tired, or have specific needs that might not be met there. In most cases, you'll be able to talk with a coordinator to see if the retreat will be able to meet your health needs. Make sure to ask some questions beforehand: Can they accommodate your specific diet? Will you have to sit for long stretches of time, and if so, how might you be able to make modifications? Can you have your own room? Let them know about your health condition well in advance and notify them of any medications you take.

For the most benefit, try to schedule a group retreat for yourself at least once a year. Retreats last anywhere from two days to two weeks.

Meditation retreats that have an embodied focus often hold a Buddhist cosmology. I've listed a few Buddhist-inspired retreats in Appendix D that are compatible with the work in this book.

The form your spiritual curriculum takes in this lifetime is ultimately between you and the guiding hand of Spirit. The purpose of True Healing is to restore wholeness to a mind that still believes it is separate from its divine source.

Since it is function over form with True Healing, any spiritual practice can be used in conjunction with the concepts in this book, as long as it fits within the framework of the True Healing principles. You should:

- Work with any method that expands its definition of healing to include the soul and not just the body.
- Use spiritual tools that help you get into your body to experience gross or subtle sensations.
- Take advantage of any practice that brings you into "the now" of the present moment.

- Find a system that teaches you to recognize the fear-based survival reactions of the ego, as well as the love-based thrival responses of Spirit.
- And above all else, adopt a practice that aims to reconnect the communication lines between yourself as Spirit, your body, and your soul.

The True Healing Ten Core Principles are bulleted on page 11. Read these over once a day and tie them around your finger as reminders on your path to True Healing.

PART IV

ILLNESS AS AN OPPORTUNITY FOR ENLIGHTENMENT

CHAPTER 16

FINDING A SPIRITUAL PURPOSE FOR ILLNESS

Defining a clear purpose for illness is one of the most intelligent ways we can incorporate life-experience within the framework of spirituality. In the practice of True Healing, we learn to work with illness rather than against it. When we work within the framework of our own karma, we grow and heal. Illness is an opportunity for growth from a spiritual perspective. We just have to learn how to see it that way.

True Healing involves alignment between the body, the soul, and Spirit. It involves alignment of purpose. Spirit creates a divine purpose for everything. Spirit even creates a purpose for the ego, albeit a temporary one: Helping us to see how much we're influenced by it. Our job isn't to make the ego go away, or even the illness, but we can always give them a purpose.

One of the very first things I look at during a medical intuition reading is the communication between the Spirit and the body. In other words, "How aligned is this person with her own spiritual information and purpose?" I read this first because a client's healing is dependent on it. As a spiritual counselor, I want to know right off the bat whether or not this person is really open to True Healing. The more a person is in alignment with her purpose, the greater her chance of healing.

Problems are harder and harder to solve if we're not aligned with our own higher purpose or at least open to accessing it. Solutions always seem to be out of reach, or we go into tremendous effort or struggle without seeming to get anywhere substantial. The lack of results can lead to a sense of defeat, fear, anger, or depression. The resulting fear catapults us into a vicious cycle that can only lead to more fear. Around and around we go like a game of cat and mouse, always chasing something but never really getting value from the effort.

When we're not aligned with our own spiritual purpose, we become reliant on other people, miracle cures, or outside information for answers. Or we put all our resources into a chosen medical modality, assuming it's going to give us everything we need to help us heal. Even people who rely on psychics, gurus, and other spiritual teachers get caught in this trap. They become reliant on a teacher's wisdom versus their own. Without knowing how to access their own supply of wisdom, they'll never see themselves as their own healers.

On the flip side, when we're aligned with our own spiritual intelligence, we have certainty in the insight it offers. We eventually trust our intuition more than we trust someone else's advice or instruction. It's not that we don't get help or take advice, but our intuition steers us in the best direction. It's able to separate the wheat from the chaff, so to speak. When aligned with purpose, the body is more and more responsive to the instruction of Spirit. Ironically, the body is happy to take Spirit's orders and will be prone to healing if it does.

A body in alignment with the purpose of Spirit is like a well-trained dog; it *wants* to take orders from a higher source. This isn't meant to be insulting to the body (or to dogs for that matter). A dog always knows its place in society. If a dog clearly recognizes someone else assigned to the position of alpha wolf, the duty of leadership, it responds enthusiastically to commands and is happy and healthy. The dog can relax because it allows its guardian to take responsibility and doesn't have to expend energy upholding a certain rank. A well-trained dog doesn't go into competition with its own guardian.

The body, too, needs to understand its role. The body's purpose is simply to listen to signals and respond to them. When it listens to signals other than Spirit—when it is off axis from its own source—it tries to take control even though it knows it can't. It takes on responsibilities it knows it isn't able to fulfill. It thinks it has to go it alone and in turn creates tremendous tension, stress, and strain for itself. But when the body remembers its role as a vehicle for Spirit and not as the driver, it is utterly relieved to hear the commands of Spirit and to follow them. It lets go of control and allows Spirit to take over. And it is happier, healthier, and holier for it.

When the body is aligned with purpose, problems aren't seen so much as problems. Instead, they are challenges to work through. Sure, with the ego around, there will always be fear, worry, and concern. It's hard to make that stuff go away. But when someone who is sick is aligned with her own truth and purpose, it's easier for her to see her illness as an opportunity for growth. The modus operandi is less about getting rid of illness and more about working with it. She wants to see her illness as purposeful. This may seem counterintuitive, but she might even have a sense of enthusiasm about it. Not that she is happy to be sick. I doubt anyone is ever happy to be sick. But she is happy to be on her path and working through something big.

Aligning illness with purpose is actually really easy. That's because purpose doesn't have to be anything other than what you want it to be. Often people hear the word "purpose" and think it must be something bigger, better, or more profound than their own inner desire. Creating a purpose is simple: what do you want your illness to be for? What do you want to learn from it? As long as you're aligned with Spirit, a purpose can be anything you want it to be. You name it, and the illness is now an opportunity versus an obstacle for True Healing.

Before I got sick, I related myself with a personality I called The Warrior Goddess. I saw myself as strong, powerful, and independent, and capable of accomplishing anything I set my mind to doing. In fact, if I wasn't *doing* something, I felt purposeless, useless, and spiritually impotent.

Looking back now, it's clear that I used doing to keep me from simply being. It was like armor on the inside of my body that kept me from entering into any relationship—including the one with myself—with a calm, peaceful abiding. I even approached my healing sessions with a kind of warrior mentality, as if my clients and I could conquer whatever needed healing.

Getting sick was my first-hand opportunity to finally just be. But it was certainly one of the hardest things I've ever done. How could I just be and still be purposeful? What use was I if I couldn't *do* anything? Just being went against my every instinct.

Recognizing my anxiety around the area of just being versus always doing, I saw my experience as a potential growth opportunity. The simple, delicate presence of beingness became the purpose of my illness. My husband and I named this mysterious unchartered aspect of myself The Priestess.

Being sick—and now also being a priestess—I had to learn how to *not* do. I stopped working and allowed my husband to financially support me, despite the nagging psychic pressure that came in from parents and grandparents (alive and dead) with strong work ethics. As a priestess, I reminded myself that I didn't have to work and imagined myself as holy enough to be fully supported by the universe. My presence was enough to heal; there wasn't anything I needed to do.

Being sick was the next step on my spiritual path. By giving it a conscious purpose, I challenged myself with a new way of being that my soul desperately desired, and I received more than I could have ever imagined in the process.

DEFINING A PURPOSE FOR ILLNESS

You get to define your illness purpose for yourself. It's not about what it "should" be or what others would have it be for you. You need to create your own reason for why. What purpose will help you grow, change, and heal?

Like change itself, your illness purpose is functional. It's not just an intention or a positive thought; it is not static. It's something that you work toward or want to bring attention to. It's something that requires practice, or something that helps you rewrite your perceptions about yourself or your illness. The purpose of your illness might actually trigger you emotionally, mentally, and spiritually; it might light up a tender area or a sore spot within you that needs healing. Growth on any level can be challenging.

The following exercise can be used as a starting point to help you find your own spiritual purpose for your illness. You'll complete the exercise in the next chapter.

FINDING YOUR ILLNESS PURPOSE
PART ONE: PAIN POINTS EXERCISE

List five to ten pain points of your illness or symptoms. These are the things you hate the most about your situation. Your pain points can include everything from physical pain to emotional pain to mental pain to financial pain.

Here are some examples of emotionally challenging pain points to get you going, although I'm sure you have many of your own:

1. I hate that I'm spending so much money on doctor bills, medications, and supplements.

2. I hate thinking that people are judging me (for my excess weight, my tired appearance, my inability to perform, etc.).

3. I hate trying to prove all the time that I'm not making it up or trying to get attention.

4. I hate feeling like I'm putting so much energy and resources into my healing and getting so little out of it.

5. I resent others for taking for granted their good health, vitality, youth, etc.

6. I hate the thought of losing my job because of all the sick days I'm taking, and for not performing how I used to.

7. I hate myself for getting this illness.

8. I hate someone *else* for giving me this illness.

9. I don't like having so much attention on me. Why can't I just be "normal"?

10. I hate being tired and having my energy zapped all the time.

You'll come back to your own specific pain points again later, so do not discard your observations. In the meantime, feel free to add to the list as you think of more.

This is the first step in finding a spiritual purpose for your illness using the emotional elements expressed through your physical body. Your purpose will help you stay on course during your process of True Healing.

CHAPTER 17

THE EMOTION OF ILLNESS

All illness involves emotion. If you're sick, you can attest to the internal surge of feelings that arise in response to the cold hard fact that illness has affected almost every aspect of your life. Maybe you had to quit your job. Maybe your creative pursuits had to be put on the back burner. Maybe your romantic or social relationships were diminished. Maybe you can't eat the foods you love. Or maybe your appearance changed and you don't fit into your clothes the way you used to. Undeniably, all of these lead to emotional responses that contribute to the bigger picture of your suffering.

Emotion is natural, literally. It's a biological response of the physical body and comes with the human package. Emotion, at its deepest, primordial core is the felt sense. The felt sense is the innate wisdom of the body-mind. It is what we meet when we get into the actual experience of the body. So as long as we're in this physical form—or unless our goal is to fight, control, or manipulate our physical existence—we'll never be able to get rid of emotions.

Yet emotions can add salt to an already suffering soul. Core feelings, the felt sense, are not the problem. The additional suffering arises with what I call secondary emotional reactions. A secondary reaction is an emotion that arises in response to the felt sense; or in other words, an emotional reaction to an emotional reaction. Secondary reactions are the stuff that keeps the wheel of karma spinning. They keep the emotional elements of illness moving through the mind, like a music track set on repeat.

Secondary emotions almost always overshadow the felt sense and the body's innate communication system. This is unfortunate because secondary reactions do not define the felt sense at all; they do not reflect what's really going on sub-surface.

Anger, rage, hatred, and resentment are perfect examples of secondary emotional reactions. I'm confident in saying that these emotions are never present at the level of the felt sense. Rather, these arise in *response* to the felt sense, from somewhere deeper than the surface of the body and mind.

If we rewind through the emotions or go deep enough into the felt sense—under the anger, let's say—we might find helplessness or hopelessness there instead. Maybe we feel helpless because it seems like we don't have any control over our situation. Lack of control might make us angry. Our anger is a secondary reaction to the original feeling of helplessness.

Or we might have an inner felt sense of abandonment, which makes us enraged that friends, family, and doctors are not showing up for us. The rage is a secondary reaction to the abandonment. A feeling-sense of disappointment may lead to hating ourselves, and a feeling-sense of confusion or fear can make us resent others for not understanding or accommodating our specific needs. The hatred and resentment arise in response to the original feelings.

The thinking mind is always involved with secondary emotional reactions, although it sometimes doesn't seem like it. Secondary reactions arise out of the thoughts we have about the underlying feelings that we're feeling. These thoughts are usually programmed in at an unconscious level. We don't realize we're *thinking* about a feeling; it happens so fast, we miss it. This is how karma is generated: our thoughts perpetuate our emotions and our emotions perpetuate our thoughts. It creates the cascading survival mode cycle we talked about in chapter three.

Let's use the helplessness example again. We don't want to feel helpless. Yet as we subconsciously sense the disturbing feeling of being helpless, thoughts arise deep in our minds about what it means to be helpless. Thoughts that generate karma are usually unconscious and are often brought on from learned experiences or memories: We remember visiting Grandpa on his deathbed or seeing the homeless guy on the street begging for change. We even remember how relieved we were that it wasn't us in those helpless situations. But then, when we find *ourselves* in one, unconscious thoughts about what it means to be helpless generate secondary emotions, like anger, anxiety, fear, worry, or panic.

Although these secondary emotional reactions can be extraordinarily uncomfortable and disturbing, they often pale in comparison to what gets exposed when we dive into the reality of the felt sense. In the zone of the felt sense, we touch into a kind of vulnerability that none of us really want to admit having. At the core, the ego knows just how fragile it really is, and doesn't want us to uncover that very fact about itself. Fully exposing ourselves to the reality of our situation often feels like free falling without a parachute.

But when we don't have the willingness to enter into the deeper felt experience of the body, all we do is blow off the steam of the secondary reactions. Processing emotions superficially—at the level of the secondary reactions—is like a perpetual pot of boiling water. We don't realize that we keep adding water to the pot. We generate more steam and keep trying to blow it off. At some point, we have to look under the lid to see what's simmering. What we find is the felt sense.

If we're always preoccupied with gross secondary reactions, we never allow ourselves to get to the heart of the pure communication that the body is trying to share with us. This communication is the gateway into the soul while we're in this physical form. The felt sense tells us what the soul thinks. Riding on top of the felt sense rather than delving deeply into it keeps us from hearing the soul's voice over the commotion of the secondary reactions.

So how do I stop these secondary reactions? Should I change my thoughts, re-envision my past, or think positively so I don't generate more karma?

That might help support you on your path, but "thinking yourself well" or trying to re-wire the mind with positive affirmations usually does not work at the level of the soul, at the level where True Healing takes place.

The problem is that, even with these kinds of well-intentioned practices, we're still not going in deep enough under the skin of the ego to really see the origin of our suffering. Trying to change our thoughts without knowing the true nature of them—where they came from and how they got there—is just another version of the same game we've been playing all along. We have to get under the superficial emotions and into the felt sense, which requires getting under our thoughts about what we find when we get there.

Your True Healing Meditation is a perfect space to work with emotion as an opportunity for growth, healing, and spiritual development. Working with emotions and the subtle feelings of the felt sense has the same practice components as working with pain or other physical symptoms. It's the same five-step practice, although this time the focus is primarily on emotion, feeling, and energy, rather than the physical qualities of the symptoms. Think of the secondary emotional reactions, and even the felt sense, as their own symptoms or expressions of karma. Emotions just come in a slightly different form than physical symptoms.

See Appendix B to work with your emotions as the fodder for the True Healing Meditation.

USING EMOTION TO DEFINE YOUR ILLNESS PURPOSE

In the last chapter, you wrote a list of pain points about your illness, the things you despise or dread about your situation. Part two of the exercise will help you continue to gather the information you need to define a spiritual purpose for the suffering you are going through at this time in your life. Part three briefly guides you through the five-step True Healing Meditation practice again, except this time using one of your emotional pain points as the theme.

Write down your observations and move on to part three when ready.

FINDING YOUR ILLNESS PURPOSE PART TWO: PAIN POINT EMOTIONS

Gather yourself in a quiet setting where you won't be disturbed for twenty to thirty minutes.

Read the first pain point you wrote down on your list from step one of the Illness Purpose Exercise.

Now think of this pain point in the emotional context of your life. Close your eyes and see if you can find the emotional element behind it. There should be a feeling that accompanies it; otherwise it wouldn't be a pain point. A pain point is painful *because* there's an emotional aspect to it.

For example, you may feel shame, fear, or self-loathing if your pain point has to do with the thought of going out in public after losing hair from your chemo treatments. You may feel frustration, self-pity, or jealousy if your pain point is related to not being able to do the things in life that used to bring you pleasure. Your pain point may be that you hate the thought of your symptoms getting worse. Does that bring up the feeling of anxiety? Or is it a genuine fear of dying?

Go through each one of your pain points and see if you can pinpoint a specific emotion or feeling that belongs to each one of them. Write down the accompanying emotion next to each pain point.

After emotionally reviewing each of your pain points, was there one or two that particularly jumped out as being core to your potential illness purpose? Look them over again and recall the emotional elements associated with them. What one or two pain points compel you? Intuitively speaking, do any seem particularly relevant to your situation? Do any of them move you deeply in some way? Does one seem to have more karma around it than the others?

You're looking for *intuitive* impulses here, not *instinctual* ones. Instinct would have you resist, run, or push back on a particularly poignant pain point. It's natural to be afraid of it. Yet intuition would have you put on your glasses and read the fine print. What is this pain point really trying to say? Is it calling to you in some way? Does it challenge you to see it as a potential purpose for your illness? Does it say, "Hey you, this is your bigger call for love"?

Take some time with this, several days if needed. Once you find a potential pain point that may hit on a purpose for your illness, move on to the next step so you can do some body-level exploration of the emotion behind the pain point. You'll take this emotion through the True Healing five steps as a means to help you define a clear purpose for your illness.

FINDING YOUR ILLNESS PURPOSE PART THREE: TRUE HEALING MEDITATION

When you think you've targeted a pain point and a corresponding emotion that might be related to your illness purpose, you're ready to explore it further via the felt sense, and ultimately to be healed by the guiding hand of Spirit.

Steps One and Two: Anchoring and scanning
Start by lying down on the floor, bed, or a couch. Lead yourself through the first two steps of the True Healing Meditation: grounding the seven anchor points and briefly scanning the four quadrants of the body.

Step Three: Go into the hotspot
Now recall the emotion that comes up when you think about your pain point. Is it fear? Worry? Remorse? Resistance? Confusion? Doubt? Sorrow? Depression? Go deeper into the body now to find the geographical location of the emotion. Where in the body most expresses

this energetic welling of emotion? Start by finding the larger area of the emotion. It might feel like a bubble or a radiating sun. It may even feel like a hole, or wind blowing through you. How big is this emotional sensation? How much of your body is experiencing it? Can you define the boundaries?

See if you can separate your thoughts about the emotion—the story that goes with the emotion—with the sensation-based experience of the emotion in the physical body. What exactly is your body doing or saying as you recall this emotion?

Try to witness, as best you can, the pure emotion just as it is. You don't have to do anything with it. It doesn't have to go away or diminish. How much can you allow the uncomfortable or disturbing sensations that come with this emotion? Stay with the raw experience of the felt sense. Notice the gross secondary sensations, as well as the underlying more subtle ones. Breathe and move from the surface down into a deeper layer, down into the ocean of your body.

Take a moment to re-anchor and imagine putting some of the karmic reactions into small river rocks or pebbles. Drop the pebbles down your anchor lines at the hips, shoulder blades, head, and feet.

Step Four: Find the call for love

What is this emotion truly asking for? From the space of the felt sense under all the secondary emotions, ask what the soul needs to take a next step in True Healing. What is the call for love? Is there a perceived lack that the body-mind is trying to express to you via this emotional sensation?

Step Five: Invite Spirit to heal

Lastly, allow yourself to receive a healing from Spirit in the form of a color vibration or sound, a feeling, an image, or a thought. Let the healing permeate your body and mind.

When you've completed the practice, sit up and take a few minutes to contemplate what happened. Specifically, ask yourself if this particular emotion, and everything that comes with it, is something you see yourself practicing with regularly. If you were to designate this pain point as a purpose for your illness—something you can use as a spiritual guide in your practice—would you be willing to allow this emotion in as you would your best friend? Does it challenge you enough? Is there enough pith to it that you could work with it long-term? Is it a pain point that you are truly moved to heal in your life?

If so, this is your illness purpose. Your pain point is now your Spirit Guide.

Close your eyes and once more recall your pain point and the corresponding emotion. See if you can now meet it with more friendliness and compassion than you could before.

Funny, isn't it? How is it that something that was once so ugly is now transformed into something so beautiful, so intentional, so functional? That's the power of a spiritual purpose for illness.

Now that you've defined your illness purpose, it's all about practicing with it. It's about recalling your emotional pain point and using that as the material for your True Healing Meditation practice.

During your practice periods, at least once each day, return to the feeling that your pain point evokes in you. Go into the felt sense and ask for your call for love. Receive a ray of color, a sound, an image, or a feeling from Spirit that can help you heal this perceived lack or need.

Continue working with this particular pain point in your True Healing Meditations until you have a distinct sense of neutrality toward it when it arises in your daily life (when the pain point doesn't have the same ability to push your buttons or trigger you in the same way it used to). There may even be a sense of compassion, understanding, friendliness, or love when faced with this particularly challenging pain point.

From here, you may want to reevaluate whether the pain point still has enough power to continue using it as your illness purpose. You may be ready for a different purpose now.

Congratulations. This is True Healing.

CHAPTER 18

FIXING VERSUS HEALING

After years of saving, Nasrudin finally had enough money to buy a new car. He scoured the lots until he found the car of his dreams. She was a beauty.

"The engine alone is worth 3K," exclaimed the salesman.

There was only one problem: The car cost $8,000, but Nasrudin only had five. He kicked the dirt as he walked off the lot.

That night, a light bulb went off in his head: "Aha!" thought Nasrudin.

First thing in the morning, he ran back to the lot and told the salesman he'd take the car without the engine.

Every time we ask to cure an illness without asking for True Healing, we end up like poor Nasrudin, tempted by a shiny new car, but without an engine to take us anywhere.

Jesus asked, "What do you benefit if you gain the whole world, but lose your own soul?" We gain nothing here if we've lost our divinity in the process. Like a car without an engine, the body gains nothing without the inclusion of Spirit. It remains an empty shell. Why bother to fix a crack in the shell if the yolk is already missing? As long as the mind and body remain devoid of Spirit, they can never truly heal, even if we stick Band-Aids all over the surface.

True Healing restores us to wholeness, to our original nature as spiritual beings. When we see ourselves as a complete manifestation of Spirit, we gain the whole world because we remember we *are* the whole world... and we don't lose any part of ourselves in the process.

Naturally, illness requires medicine for healing. But instead of solving the error at the core—at the level of the yolk or the engine—the ego's prescription for illness is to patch the cracks in the shell, the body. Yet putting a stopgap on physical symptoms doesn't mean we've reached into the very nature of the problem. Fixing the illness in the body doesn't mean we've healed the illness in the soul.

Attempts to fix the body without healing the separation of the soul are everywhere in Western medicine. We take pills to fix our symptoms, then more pills to fix the symptoms that the other pills caused. Pretty soon, we have a cabinet full of pills, and we can't even remember what the original pill was for.

There's also the "just take it out" formula. We've become so accustomed to removing anything that expresses symptoms, we get rid of it without exploring why it wasn't working in the first place.

I'm reminded of a tall tale about a woman who went to her doctor to get treated. The doctor asked if she'd had any surgeries. "Yes", she replied. "I had an ache in the right, so they took out my gall bladder. I had an ache in the left, so they took out my colon. I had an ache in the middle, so they took out my uterus." The doctor acknowledged the mess she was in: "Whatever you do, don't tell them you have an ache in the head."

These quick-fix methods for the body may eliminate some of our immediate pains or illnesses, but they often do not create lasting results at the soul-level. When we focus on patching holes at the surface, we skim over our situation without looking deeply at the truth of what's underneath. This could be called spiritual bypassing.

Bypassing doesn't just concern Western medicine; even formulas that look spiritual on the outside—meditation, recitation of mantras, positive thinking, affirmations—can be a form of spiritual bypassing. If someone wants only to fix the body but lacks the desire to heal the original error, what real and lasting effect could it have?

Of course, the desire to be pain-free is a natural human response to illness. No one wants to feel bad. It's not that we have to shut out our desire to be free of sickness in order for True Healing to happen. In fact, the desire to be well is the inertia we need for spiritual healing. Our deepest desire to be healed wells up from our innate spiritual wisdom. As souls, we naturally want to move back into wholeness and to reconnect with everything that is and ever will be. *That's* healing, and is the most intelligent choice we could ever make. Without desire, we'd be stuck with the ego, stuck in separation, un-whole and unhealed, for eternity.

The problem starts when the ego takes control of our desire to be whole. Like a game of pin the tail on the donkey, the ego blindfolds us and allows us to stick this desire anywhere else but on the horse's ass. It turns the desire to know who we are as Spirit into the desire to control outcomes, to make everything go the way we presume it should go. It keeps us fixated on what we think success or failure is and keeps us coming back for more until we've determined that we've solved the big puzzle.

The ego will never let us solve this puzzle! This process would last forever if the ego had its way. The ego never has the real solution for us in mind. If it did, we'd all have hopped the return flight home to Spirit long ago, and the ego would have disappeared in the contrails.

Ironically, the more we release our grip and the less we try to control outcomes, we feel safer and more supported in the world. Spirit carries us forward. When we give the healing back to the hands of Spirit, Spirit effortlessly leads us to our real solutions, to our True Healing. The body knows how to listen to the call of Spirit; when Spirit is given permission to enter, the body naturally responds and heals.

Yet, fixing illness in the body isn't actually the point of True Healing. Spirit has bigger intentions. It wants to heal you from the inside out. It wants you to understand who you are and where you truly come from.

TRUSTING YOUR PATH

Those of us who are sick or injured have a golden opportunity for True Healing. Signs of "soul sickness," of separation, are very obvious to us; they are in our faces every day in the form of pain, fatigue, stress, fear, and anguish. Sickness gives us the opportunity to notice. My definition of a courageous soul is someone who is on a spiritual path and who suffers with physical or emotional trauma, debilitating injury, or chronic illness. Rather than falling behind, these souls are forging ahead. They are willing to manifest exaggerated, outward expressions of a deeper disease inside the collective consciousness. In truth, if one person is sick, the entire population is sick. Have you considered that, by way of your illness, you may be healing yourself and all of humanity?

Tibetan Buddhist nun Pema Chodron says, "What's happening is the path to enlightenment." Nothing more and nothing less is needed. Even our most sick or painful experiences hold within themselves tremendous potential for True Healing. In simply witnessing any experience for what it is, just as it is, without gripping, forcing, or manipulating, we have full and complete access to the mind of Spirit that underlies it all.

I used to think that the more enlightened I became, the more the world would lay down its jacket while I tiptoed across the parted Red Sea without getting seaweed stuck in my toes. It was a rude awakening to discover that "bad" and uncomfortable situations would still occur. I was doing all the right things. Shouldn't I be rewarded or at least thanked for it?

Well, that never happened. Instead, I experienced the exact situations I needed in every moment to help me heal. This included pain, illness, doubt, and depression.

The resource of healing is always there; we hold the prescription. Through the muse of illness, True Healing creates lasting results that the separated soul can carry through this lifetime and throughout eternity. True Healing provides growth, learning, expansion, and exploration as the soul begins its return to Spirit, its return to wholeness.

The more willingness we have to explore and understand our current manifestation of suffering—and its true origins—the easier it is to heal.

Spirit says: "Trust this process. You'll learn something from it." It never says: "Run from this. It will kill you."

The source of any miracle cannot come from the body, a certain practice, a special pill, or a renowned physician. Our sole responsibility lies in giving ourselves the space to listen deeply to what we need. Spirit will provide the rest.

The miracle of True Healing isn't harder to attain than any other. To Spirit, all miracles are one and the same. If True Healing is an expression of love, which it is, it is inevitable. You are bound for miracles. You are on a path leading home.

AFTERWORD

FILLING THE CRACKS WITH GOLD

At one point while writing *True Healing*, something began to gnaw at me; something kept me from going forward with the writing. I felt stuck and unsure about myself, as well as the direction of the book. I stopped, laid myself down on the floor, and went into the True Healing Meditation to work through this creative block in the most embodied way I could.

In a near instant after inviting my soul to share its call for love—the real need underlying this block—I heard and felt the words, "It needs a purpose." Of course, I knew exactly what "it" was: the book itself needed a really good reason to be here. Without an understanding of the true purpose of the book, I'd have little inspiration to keep writing.

I saw an image of a broken piece of pottery that had been repaired with an inlay of gold. This is the Japanese art of kintsugi. In kintsugi, once an object has been broken, it has a history, its own story. Because of its imperfection, it has something special to share with the world. And it is more beautiful because of it.

I knew what the image was telling me. The book would help people find something valuable, maybe even beautiful, out of a broken circumstance. *True Healing* offers a chance to finally notice that the wholeness of Spirit underlies every seemingly hopeless or helpless situation.

The world of bodies and egos will never be perfect. It will always be broken. But the ability to recognize Spirit between the cracks keeps us moving toward our completion as souls. It keeps us moving toward True Healing.

APPENDIX A

THE ABBREVIATED TRUE HEALING MEDITATION

Start your practice lying down on the floor or a bed with knees up, or in any position that is most comfortable for you. Set aside thirty minutes for your practice period.

Get audio versions of the True Healing Meditation at TrueHealingBook.com
Enter password: thrival

Step One: Anchor your body

Make an energetic connection from the seven anchor points all the way down into the central core of the planet. The anchor points are located at the two sit bones, the two shoulder blades, the back of the head, and both feet. Allow stored karma in the form of tension, pain, fatigue, intense emotions, or energy around these areas to release by imagining yourself putting the energy into river rocks or pebbles. Drop the pebbles down your anchor lines.

Step Two: Scan the quadrants

Briefly run your awareness through the body to get a keener sense of where you are storing karma. Scan the feet, calves, and thighs (quad one); the pelvis, hips, and belly (quad two); the chest, shoulders, upper back, and arms (quad three); and the neck, face, and head (quad four). Look for pockets of pain, tension, stress, or intense emotion, and then pick one specific area for deeper exploration. Finish step two by dropping some pebbles down your anchor lines to release stored karma.

Step Three: Go into the hotspot

Start to feel into the area of your choice that is holding karma. Get a sense of the breadth and depth of the sensation, where it starts and where it ends. Describe the texture and quality of it, and find the emotional element that accompanies the physical nature of this hotspot. See if you can engage the felt sense, the aggregation of sensation, feeling, and vibration underneath the conscious mind. Finish step three by dropping some pebbles down your anchor lines to release stored karma.

Step Four: Find the call for love

Staying with the direct experience of the body rather than the thinking mind, ask yourself what your soul believes it is lacking right now—the real need that underlies the pain or symptom. State your question with a phrase, like, "What is my call for love?" or a mental image like a question mark or an open book. Allow the answer to come in its own way, on its own time. You may get a word or phrase, a feeling sense, or a gestalt-like knowing, in which you intuitively understand the answer "off the top of your head".

Step Five: Invite Spirit to Heal

Now ask Spirit to give you a vibrational healing in the form of color, light, sound, feeling, presence, imagery, or a thought that fulfills the perceived lack. You might see this in your mind's eye, feel it in your body, or just know it off the top of your head. Ask Spirit to fill your mind with that particular healing vibration. Allow Spirit to send it anywhere in your body that needs it. Notice where the healing goes and how it affects your body, mind, and emotional state.

Complete the practice by dropping some pebbles down your anchor lines to release stored karma. Gently sit up, take a deep breath, and move on with your day.

APPENDIX B

FEELING AS FODDER FOR THE FIVE STEPS

This exercise focuses on an emotion—rather than a physical symptom—as the target hotspot for the True Healing Meditation. You can come into the practice in one of three ways: 1) when there's an emotion welling and you'd like to work with that particular emotion in a practice setting; 2) you're working with a certain emotional theme as your illness purpose; or 3) you want to work with any emotion that arises while scanning the body in the present moment.

Steps One and Two: Anchoring and scanning

Start with anchoring the seven points at the sit bones, shoulder blades, head, and feet. Then scan the quadrants (legs, hips, chest, and head) to help you get into your body and move deeper into the felt sense.

Step Three: Go into the emotional hotspot

Emotional expression is most obvious in the torso area, around the subtle energy centers of the body—the pelvis, belly, solar plexus, chest, and throat.

If you already have a particular emotion coming up that you want to work with specifically, start by locating the part of the body that seems to be expressing the emotion. See if you can actually locate the emotion inside your body.

Then go into the hotspot of the emotion, just as you'd explore a physical symptom in step three of the practice. What temperature does the emotion have? How big is it? How much space does it take up? Does it have a texture and quality to it? Sinking? Expanding? Heaviness? Weightiness? How does it affect your physical body? Do you notice a physical component to the emotion? Tension? Stress? Holding? Pain? Fatigue?

See if you can experience the emotion just as it is without judging it. It's less about what you think about the emotion and more about simply getting into the body and feeling the pure emotion itself. You may even sense the energetics of the emotion. There's a raw experience to this. That rawness is the felt sense.

Step Four: Find the call for love

Just as you would when working with a physical hotspot, ask yourself what your soul believes it is lacking right now. What is the real need in present-time that underlies this emotional uprising? What is the soul's call for love? Stay with the felt-experience of the body to receive your answer.

Step Five: Invite Spirit to heal

Now ask Spirit to give you a vibrational healing in the form of a color, feeling, thought, or sound that fulfills the perceived lack on the soul-level. Open your mind and body to this healing and notice how it affects your body, mind, and emotional state.

Refocus on the emotional hotspot and see if you can greet it with more equanimity and compassion. The emotion may still be there, but notice if you are able to say hello to it with more allowance and neutrality.

APPENDIX C

TRUE HEALING MEDITATION Q AND A

I resist my daily practice and sometimes skip it altogether. Is there something I can do to make the resistance go away?

Resistance is usually a secondary reaction to fear, and fear doesn't feel good. Ever. Your resistance comes from the ego; it's there so you don't have to feel the fear. If you resist, you'll likely walk away rather than sit with the fear, and then you don't have to actually *be* with it.

The best way I know to work with resistance is to make it a part of the practice. It's just another sensation that's arising. It's something you can explore. Once you become comfortable with the fact that your practice is about experiencing whatever arises, resistance becomes less of a problem. It's just what you happen to be meditating with today. "Today I'm meditating with resistance because today resistance is what is showing up."

That said, in no case should the practice create more stress for you. If a tremendous amount of resistance arises regarding your practice, take a step back. Take a few days or weeks off. Let the intensity wane a little and then resume when some of the energy has cleared.

I struggle to stay present with my body in my practice. Is there something I can do?

Wandering in and out of the body is natural and normal. As a soul, you are pure light and cannot be confined to a limited physical space. Yet the practice is to come into the body to witness your reactions and sensations.

No one expects you to stay inside the body always. If you can touch in for a few seconds to a few minutes at a time, you're doing fine. The more you practice, the longer you'll be able to hold your awareness on the body.

As soon as you recognize that you have wandered from the body, first just acknowledge "where" you are. Are you in a daydream? Are you thinking ahead into the future or back into the past? Without judging that experience, come back to scanning the body. Use your anchor lines to help you ground. No matter what step you were doing before going unconscious, go back to feeling the sensations arising in the body. Then go back to particular step you were in before you drifted off.

I fall asleep while practicing. Is this okay?

The lying-down posture can sometimes induce sleep because it's the most relaxing of all meditation postures. If you are exhausted or under stress or duress, which illness or injury creates, it is not uncommon to fall asleep while practicing. This might not be a bad thing. Your practice periods might be the only time when you can get any restful sleep.

You may also be in a spiritual growth period and releasing deeper layers of unconscious karma in the body. During a growth period, remaining present with your experience may be more difficult.

In both of these circumstances, don't sweat falling asleep during practice. Of course, sleeping shouldn't be the intention of the practice, but if you do find yourself falling asleep, don't struggle to stay awake. While sleeping, you will unconsciously practice and will do the work on the soul-level. You might even feel revitalized when you wake up.

I spend too much time scanning the body and don't have time to do the final steps. Should I skip a step or do it faster?

Everyone practices at their own pace. With practice, you'll find your tempo and will be able to move through the entire exercise in about thirty minutes. You may find that you like more time to anchor and scan the body and less time for the healing work. Or you might prefer it the other way around.

If you've been practicing awhile and are still not finding enough time to do the complete exercise in a timely manner, you might be getting fixated on a particular step. You might think you have to get the step perfect or to clear something or to feel something particular before moving on. You don't have to feel anything special before going on. All you need to do is feel your body right now. Some days you'll feel more, other days less. Part of the meditation path is in knowing that the body will never be perfect. It's impossible to be a perfect meditator.

Keeping your attention moving through the steps will help you from getting fixated. A good practice to bust fixation and the "perfection game" is to consciously move to the next step even if it doesn't feel quite perfect.

I can't feel anything or make anything happen in my practice periods. Isn't something supposed to happen?

The number one goal for the practice is to spend time in your body witnessing sensations, emotions, and energy arising and passing. If something is "supposed" to happen, it's just you getting into your body. If you try to make something happen, you probably are not allowing yourself to be present with your body, and you are missing the purpose of the practice. It's about witnessing what is, not about trying to make something that *isn't* happening happen.

True Healing is a long-term process that occurs by taking baby steps. One layer at a time, you'll peel your karmic onion. You likely will not have profound spiritual revelations in most of your daily practice periods. I surely don't. If you feel a conscious energetic shift in just one of your sessions every week or two, that's a good gauge that you are progressing on your path of True Healing.

APPENDIX D

TRUE HEALING RESOURCES

With the purchase of *True Healing,* you have free access to the audio versions of the True Healing Meditation outlined in the book. I highly recommend that you make use of the audio to learn the practices. Access the audio files at the *True Healing* website, **TrueHealingBook.com.** Use the password: **thrival**.

FURTHER WORK WITH ALISON ANTON

I offer a variety of courses and services for people who struggle with illness—and for the healers who work with them—through my online school, Anton Guild of Spiritual Medicine. Visit **AntonGuild.com** for more information on my offerings, including:

- Group Healings and Meditations
- Your Mind Is Your Medicine Course
- Medical Intuition Readings
- Clairvoyant Training
- Workshops and Retreats

PROGRAMS AND RETREATS

True Healing Home Retreat
Alison Anton, Anton Guild of Spiritual Medicine
AntonGuild.com | TrueHealingBook.com

Meditating with the Body Retreat
Reginald A. Ray, Dharma Ocean
DharmaOcean.org

Insight Meditation Retreats
Spirit Rock Meditation Center | SpiritRock.org
Insight Meditation Society | Dharma.org

REFERENCES

A Course in Miracles. Foundation for Inner Peace. (Foundation for Inner Peace, 1975).

The Biology of Belief—Unleashing the Power of Consciousness, Matter and Miracles. Bruce Lipton. (Sounds True, Inc., 2006).

The Disappearance of the Universe. Gary R. Renard. (Hay House, Inc., 2004).

Feeding Your Demons—Ancient Wisdom for Resolving Inner Conflict. Tsultrim Allione. (Little, Brown and Company, 2008).

Focusing. Eugene Gendlin. (Bantam New Age Books, 1978).

Healing the Unhealed Mind. Kenneth Wapnick. (Temecula: Foundation for A Course in Miracles, 2011.)

How to Be Sick—A Buddhist-Inspired Guide for the Chronically Ill. Toni Bernhard. (Wisdom Publications, 2010).

Meditating with the Body Retreat Program. Reginald A. Ray. (Dharma Ocean, 2005).

Mindfulness Meditation for Pain Relief—Guided Practices for Reclaiming Your Body and Your Life. Jon Kabat-Zinn. (Sounds True, Inc., 2010.)

New Beliefs, New Brain—Free Yourself from Stress and Fear. Lisa Wimberger. (Divine Arts Media, 2012).

Reinventing the Body, Resurrecting the Soul—How to Create a New You. Deepak Chopra. (Three Rivers Press, 2009).

Touching Enlightenment—Finding Realization in the Body. Reginald A. Ray. (Sounds True, Inc., 2008).

When Things Fall Apart—Heart Advice for Difficult Times. Pema Chodron. (Shambhala Publications, Inc., 1997).

IN GRATITUDE

Imagine you're a professional editor. One day a first-time spiritual-self-help author plops a manuscript on your desk. The author thinks the book is pretty great as it is. "It just needs a little fine-tuning and a good spell check," she says.

I was said author.

My impressions about *True Healing* were blown—in an extraordinary way—by my editor's masterful eye the very first day she got her fingers on it. Sarah Shifferd not only helped me with the necessary development and all the editing, she taught me how to write a book. I think Sarah and I are the only ones who really know how far this book came in the year it took to write and edit it. I thank her from the bottom of my heart for her major contribution, from conception to completion.

I also want to thank Kelly Notaras, Jeffrey Allen, and Raphaelle Tamura for their insights early on in the development of the book. I am utterly grateful for their professional and spiritual eyes.

I am blessed to have a multi-media design guru as a husband. Jackson Carson has created so many websites and promotional materials for me that I've lost count. He was always behind me, beside me, and sometimes in front of me when it came to the creative and spiritual support for *True Healing*. Jackson very literally was the cornerstone that made this book happen. I'm so grateful for the lovely book cover and website.

I have also had many wonderful, dedicated spiritual teachers in this lifetime that have helped shape my own teaching and the content of this book. I can only hope to affect others as deeply as they have touched me.

Editing Support

Sarah Shifferd, SarahKShifferd.com

Kelly Notaras, KNLiterary.com

Creative and Design Support

Jackson Carson, JacksonDCarson.com

ABOUT THE AUTHOR

Alison Anton has been teaching and practicing the art of energy medicine, meditation, and spiritual healing since 1995. She is the founder of Anton Guild of Spiritual Medicine, where she offers online body-mind courses and healing services for people struggling with chronic illness. The Guild also has an advanced clairvoyant program and medical intuition training for professional healers. Alison's other works include, *Your Mind Is Your Medicine* audio course and *What Color Is Your Bubble? Children's Tools for Intuition* CD set for kids.

Alison has been a practitioner of *A Course in Miracles* since 1997. These practices in forgiveness—as well as her energy medicine work, embodied meditation, and silent retreats—have influenced every step in her personal and spiritual life.

Alison's vision is to help people who struggle with chronic, debilitating, or terminal illness understand the spiritual dimensions of health and disease. Her goal is to heal the split between the Spirit, the soul, and the physical body.

Visit Alison's website for more information about her offerings: **AntonGuild.com**

42218934R00122

Made in the USA
Charleston, SC
20 May 2015